AF572353

THE LAST TRUMP

by

H.L. McLEAN

EPIPHANY PUBLICATIONS

Berkley, Michigan

First Printing September 1990
Library of Congress Catalog Card Number: 90-82592
ISBN 0-9627225-0-2

A HERALD OF THE KING

H.L. McLEAN

CONTENTS

The Last Trump

PREFACE

OH GREAT! Just what the world needs - Yet another book on Biblical Prophecy by some 'wild-eyed' preacher with a private pipeline of spiritual information discernable only by meticulous observation of the Urim and Thummim.

Ahhh yesss...well, not quite!!! First of all, this book is not intended for everyone in the 'world', but for people who want a clearer understanding of how biblical prophecy relates to historical, current, and future events.

Secondly, this writer is not a 'wild-eyed preacher'. In fact, you may well note the absence of three points and a poem in any of the ensuing chapters. Moreover, this writer is neither a preacher, minister, evangelist, pastor, teacher, apostle or missionary!

Thirdly, my pipeline is about 95% perspiration and 5% inspiration. I don't possess any 'peekstone' or have special access to an 'angel', nor do I receive any special 'vibrations' from ether waves.

Fourthly, I don't believe there is a any 'hocus pocus' about Bible interpretation. It is rather, a very pragmatic literal understanding of the text in question, regardless of any personal feelings or doctrinal position. This approach sometimes causes difficulty because one must change his thinking to fit what the Bible is teaching. That may sound quite elementary, but if you continue reading, you may find that you need to do some 'soul searching' with your theology also.

This book reflects a record of my personal search for the truth regarding a proper understanding of the Word of God as it is applied to significant prophetic events that may soon be coming to pass, the most significant of which is the second coming of 'Messiah'. In the process of the investigation as to 'when' the Lord Jesus would return, I encountered a number of topics that are intrinsically intertwined with the second advent that needed to be analyzed as well. I had initially begun the investigation over a decade ago to prove conclusively to myself that the Pretribulation Theology that I had espoused for so many years, could be demonstrated to my satisfaction by a thorough examination of the Scriptures. One approach I used was to examine the four Greek words that were used in relation to Christ's second coming.[1] If I could prove that 'parousia' always referred to the Lord's coming 'for the Church', and 'apokalupsis' always meant 'coming in judgement', and 'epiphany' referred to the Lord's 'coming in glory', then I would have a legitimate argument to support my pretrib position. If you have ever done this study, then you can surmise the outcome. I could not demonstrate the veracity of this theory to my satisfaction, and subsequently, had to retract my theory, at least temporarily, until I could prove beyond a shadow of doubt that the Lord was indeed coming before the Tribulation started. Because of the difficulty I had in demonstrating my position, I refrained from teaching on prophecy from that time on until now, even after repeated requests. I had always thought my hermeneutics to be quite adequate for proper bible interpretation, and highly subscribed to well

[1] **παρουσια, αποκαλυψισ, ερχομαι, επιφανεια**

accepted orthodox guides such as Ramm[2] I did not realize that I was really 'reading into' the scriptures, that which I had 'hoped' it was saying as I was searching the Word for information regarding the coming of the Lord. I recently returned to the study, as a result of the prodding of a friend who wanted me to determine if the Lord was returning in September 1988. I determined that the 'colander theory' was incorrect several weeks before the suggested timing occurred, but in resuming the study, I became determined once again, to settle the matter to my own satisfaction. Much of the contents of that study are to be found in this book, and may be somewhat difficult to accept for a 'pretribber'.

---

[2] Ramm, *Protestant Biblical Interpretation*

1.

PROLEGOMENON

This 'Prolegomenon' is an extended introduction and overview of the contents, philosophy, and reasons behind the material in this book.

Prophetic material

A recent visit to one of my favorite bible book stores was a rather disturbing revelation to me. Where I once found an 'island' crammed with a variety of books on bible prophecy, I now found only two small rows of outdated prophetic material in the very back of the store. This surprised me considerably, so I proceeded to make my way to the commentary section, with hopes of finding additional material in that department. I discovered, rather alarmingly, that there were only a few very dated commentaries on Revelation. When my own private collection of prophetic books approaches that of my favorite bible book store, something is definitely wrong. Space apparently is not the problem, because there are several complete islands dedicated to christian cups, glasses, and greeting cards. There are of course several islands dedicated to 'christian' tapes and records, and several complete islands are dedicated to 'spiritual life' aids. You can learn all about the blessings of speaking in tongues, or using psychology in marriage and dating. There are autobiographical books by TV personalities, and books to tell you how to make money or loose weight. Who is blowing the trumpet? Who is warning people about the impending conditions so carefully delineated in the holy word? Doesn't anybody care, or am I over reacting?

my interest in prophecy

My interest in prophecy goes back to childhood, when at about the age of 7 or 8, my friend's dad said something like "It says in the Bible that the Russians are going to rule the world". This man was not a 'Bible Scholar' by any sense of the imagination, but his statement aroused a curiosity that seemed to stick. Forty years later, I still think about what he said, and wonder 'what does the Bible say about what is going to happen in my generation'? It was a Bible preacher that was teaching through the book of Revelation that caused me, at the age of 19 to attend a Seventh Day Adventist church on Sunday evenings to hear what the Bible had to say about the future. I was so uninformed about religion, that I didn't even realize that Seventh Day Adventists don't even have services on Sunday! It so happened that the preacher was from a group that didn't have a building, and was temporarily using the Adventist's facilities. The preacher was explaining things from the book of Revelation that I had never heard before, that I didn't understand, but which aroused a curiosity and an overwhelming compulsion to understand. Here I was in the midst of a church full of people that carried their bibles, and knew what was written in them, and I didn't know the difference between King James and C.I. Scoffield. This was exceedingly humiliating to my philosophical ego, and I determined that I should be able to understand what it was all about too, so I started to read a New Testament Bible until I came to this passage:

Rom.10:9,10

> *That if you confess with your mouth Jesus as Lord, and believe in your heart that God raised Him from the dead, you shall be saved; for with the heart man believes, resulting in righteousness,and with the mouth he confesses, resulting in*

salvation.

I really didn't know what it meant to 'be saved', or what it meant to 'go forward for salvation', or any of the other jargon of 'believers', because it wasn't part of my heritage. All I knew was what the book said, and I said 'Lord I believe', and something happened. I wasn't sure at the time what had taken place, but I knew something was different, and it became more obvious as time went on. Christianity was not after all, a 2000 year old philosophy of religion, but rather a personal relationship with the living Lord Jesus Christ. If the terms 'born again' and 'saved' make you feel uncomfortable, and you can't express with certainty that you absolutely know you are a 'born again' christian, then you need to have a conversion experience before you go any farther in this book.

what does it mean to be a christian

I have heard people say that they have 'always been a christian', and while I don't mean any disrespect, that isn't the way it works. A person isn't born by natural birth into the kingdom of God anymore than a person is born automatically married to another person. Becoming a christian has a great similarity to a marriage ceremony, where there is a mutual consent and a mutual promise. In our case the Lord has already spoken His part of the wedding vow, and the onus of responsibility is now left to us. Will you have this Man to be your Lord and Savior? He leaves it up to you!

six personalities

There are going to be six personalities or 'players' in the third and final act of this age, and they will be:

1.) Antichrist
2.) False Prophet
3.) Satan
4.) Moses
5.) Elijah
6.) The Lord Jesus Christ

This book contains a considerable amount of information about the identity of the **'Antichrist'**, and should be of some value in identifying his soon appearance. He will be a specific individual that will emulate many of the things of Christ, even his death and resurrection.

The **'False Prophet'** is a person who suggests that people worship the antichrist or his image, and he reminds me of a secretary of state that is the official representation of a president. His authority rests with the other individual.

'Satan' will personally take possession of the antichrist. Over zealous 'spiritual' christians have often been carried away chasing the devil around. I only see one illustration in the entire Bible that Satan personally took possession of a person, and that person was Judas Iscariot. The scripture is clear; "And Satan entered into Judas who was called Iscariot..."(Luke 22:3). It may well be that he has personally taken possession of others also, the scriptures just doesn't specifically say so. I think he will personally poses Antichrist based on the context of (Rev.13).

I call prophet no.1 **'Moses'**, but the scripture doesn't specifically give him a name. I refer to him by that name because of the similarity of the plagues of Egypt during the Exodus, and the seven bowls of wrath during the tribulation as revealed in Revelation. He will be an individual man who will be used by the Lord to prophesy for 3 1/2 years, and to turn the waters to blood and smite the earth with every plague as often as he desires.

I call prophet no.2 **'Elijah'**, because one of the things that Elijah did was to stop the rain from falling, and these two prophets have that same power. (Rev.11:6). Furthermore, there is a specific prophecy about Elijah coming before the Lord returns;

Mal.4:5,6

Prolegomenon

Behold, I am going to send you Elijah the prophet before the coming of the great and terrible day of the LORD. And he will restore the hearts of the fathers to their children, and the hearts of the children to their fathers, lest I come and smite the land with a curse.

The O.T. prophets were Hebrews, and one would suspect that these last two prophets would be also. They are called 'olive trees', and 'lampstands' (Rev.11:4), and are identical to the olive trees and lampstands of (Zech. 4:3). However, churches are also called 'lampstands' (Rev.1:20), and gentile believers are called 'wild olive' branches that have been grafted into the root of the natural olive tree (Rom.11:17). It is also to be noted that the salvation that has come to the gentiles, has come to make Israel jealous (Rom.11:11). What would make the Jews more jealous than to have a verified prophet sent from God to prophesy to them with the undisputable sanction of God, and have him be a gentile? This is purely conjuncture on my part, but it is an interesting one. Few evangelical churches today have an office of a prophet, even though prophecy itself, is not an uncommon phenomenon. We don't have any problems with apostles, evangelists, pastors, and teachers, but how many churches do you know of that also have people who act as prophets? It would not surprise me to discover these two prophets coming from a gentile evangelical background, although it is highly improbable.

about the book

This book is a result of a study which began at the request of a friend who asked me to investigate the veracity of several books which placed a September 1988 date for the return of the Lord and the rapture of the church. As a result of this unusual request, I resumed a previous study concerning the rapture, which was begun over a decade ago, that attempted to positively demonstrate that pretribulational theology was the most scripturally correct. The more I studied, the more I realized that much of my eschatology was 'adopted' from other peoples 'ideas' on the interpretation of certain passages. Whenever I studied these certain passages, I automatically 'read into them' the already formulated concepts that I had previously adopted. We all do this to some extent, without even realizing that we are accepting interpretation even when we think we are doing original bible study work. This seems especially true of reference bibles that have annotated comments on rather difficult portions that we are uninformed about, and some of these are extremely valuable and helpful tools that are normally very profitable for our use and spiritual maturity. I used one very popular reference bible for 10 years, and felt it was the most influential and helpful guides of my earlier christian learning experience. When I was a young boy growing up in a very small town in a remote area of Michigan's upper peninsula, many words and phrases that I learned, were what we call 'colloquial' expressions. They were frequently used expressions, accents, and words that were understood by everybody, except that they could never be found in a dictionary because it was not 'correct english'. 'Jaeet cher suppr' may be perfectly understood as 'did you eat your supper', but most certainly would not be considered acceptable English. Much of our theology is learned in a similar manner in which we adopt the things we have heard and learned from the people we associate with, the churches we attend, the preachers we listen to, the bibles we read and etc. Indeed, the scripture reflects this learning experience in many places by stating "...and how shall they believe in Him whom they have not heard? And how shall they hear without a preacher?" (Rom.10:14). Most sects, and denominations have arisen from 'colloquial' interpretations of scripture, and I am convinced much of our evangelical theology is adopted in a similar manner. Unfortunately, most of us have neither the time nor the facility to explore topics of this nature to the depth they require to develop satisfactory conclusions, which even at best, are controversial anyway. Consequently we adopt the theology of our teachers, regardless if that teaching is formal or not. I believe everyone who has thought about theology at all has a 'philosophy of religion' that he has developed or taken upon himself. That philosophy may be nearly anything from science fiction to realism, from secular humanism to theism, from modernism to neo-orthodoxy. Most people have developed some sort of philosophy whether they realize it or not, because It's inherent in the nature of man.

Many of us like to visualize both history and prophecy step by step, minute by minute, inch by inch, in some type of chronological table or ticking clock where each tick marks a period of time towards the end of the age. We picture a yard stick seven years long, marked off in increments of time, and divided in the middle with a big mark indicating 3 & 1/2 years. As time goes by, the world seemingly rolls down the edge of this scale, mark by mark, year by year, gaining momentum as it rolls faster and faster to its own demise. While this may be a convenient method of visualizing prophecy, it really doesn't do justice to the prophetic unfolding of the plan of God. Perhaps a better visual aid would be to imagine the sequence of prophetic unfolding as a gigantic chessboard, where the pieces vary in significance, power, and range. Some pieces lurking in the back row can suddenly strike across the entire board in one move while others must move only one square, and that in a specific direction. In this chess game, however, we must imagine a four dimensional chess board with levels that go back through time to the very beginning. Consider that there are many concurrent events happening at the same time at different levels in this fourth dimensional game, some of which transcend their layer and emerge on the bottom, which is the only one we can physically see. Each square of our chessboard marks out an arena of spiritual conflict which ultimately will bring us to the threshold of eternity. I have listed a few of these major arenas of conflict:

1.) ***The Church***:

We are probably most familiar with this one, since it is the one that most directly affects us as believers. We can look back to its origin at Pentecost, and see changes throughout its history. There have been times of revival, and times of persecution; times of darkness and times of enlightenment; times of sadness and times of joy; times of pride and times of embarrassment; times of poverty and times of abundance.

It has a *commission* (Mt.28:19,20).
to make disciples, baptize and teach.

It has a *comfort* (Mt.28:20).
"I am with you always".

It has a *promise* (Mt.16:18).
The gates of hell shall not overpower it.

It has *spiritual authority* (Mt.16:19; Lk.10:19,20)
to tread upon serpents, (the works of the Devil).

It has a *future* (Jn.14:1-3)
"...I go to prepare a place for you..."

2.) ***Israel:***

Since God called Abraham from Ur of the Chaldees, Israel has been a people through whom God has chosen to reveal His name, His praise, and His glory (Jer.13:11), and even though they are presently in partial darkness, they play the major role in the unfolding of prophecy. This arena of spiritual conflict is going to increase in intensity and frequency until the whole world is embroiled in a conflagration that ultimately becomes the birth pains of Israel's spiritual birth, and the dawn of a new age in the history of mankind.

3.) ***Human government:***

The powers that be are ordained of God, and they are not there by accident or quirk of fate. We are told to pray for our leaders that we may lead a quiet and peaceful life. Somehow behind the political scene there are angels who have been given the responsibility for the historical direction of nations, and there are opposing spiritual forces that try and get the nation moving in a direction away from God. Paul refers to this arena of struggle in Ephesians 6 by referring to the evil forces as principalities and powers that we wrestle against.

4.) ***Believers***:
Within every true believer there is a spiritual dichotomy that reflects a conflict between good and evil, which ultimately reflects the ongoing conflict between The Lord Jesus and Satan. It is a struggle between the old nature and the Holy Spirit, which cohabits every believer, and the winner is the one that we ultimately yield to. Paul explains the rudiments of this personal struggle in Ephesians chapter 6.

5.) ***Heaven***:
There is going to be a tremendous battle in the heavens by spirit beings which will take place sometime during the span of the seven year tribulation period. This arena will feature Satan and his angels on one side, and Michael and his angels on the other side. Satan will ultimately loose the battle, will be ousted from heaven, and will be thrown down to earth with great wrath, see (Rev.12:7).

the mechanism

I have used the ellipsis (3 dots...) to indicate a partial quotation; quotation marks (" ") to indicate an exact quotation; and the apostrophe quotes (' ') are used for emphasis. I have intentionally abbreviated the footnotes and placed the complete footnote reference in a bibliography section, which is intended to permit a reader to verify the authenticity of the annotated subject material. I have tried to keep the context of each chapter indigenous to that chapter, but this is nearly impossible because every area of prophetic study overlaps into other related areas.

I have used the NASV (New American Standard Version) of the Bible nearly exclusively for the quotations within the book, as it is the version that I personally prefer for my own Bible studies.

of tigers and men

It may be observed that my opinions expressed in this book are of a modified post tribulational viewpoint and are somewhat biased at the expense of other views, and thus constitute what might be alluded to as a 'paper tiger'. In addition to this technique, I also occasionally set up the logic for an obvious conclusion, which some might term a 'straw man'.

It is not my intention to denigrate in any way the scholarship of views other than my own. The fact of the matter is that I am deeply indebted to the scholarship of many godly men, whose works of exegesis have greatly enriched my own personal development. I hope the efforts herein do not reflect any 'ad hominem' arguments to support my conclusions, but rather an introspective view of my own exegetical studies.

what do you know?

Perhaps a better expression would be 'what can you know?'. Many people know for sure that nobody else can know something that they don't. This reminds me of the Chaldeans who were called before king Nebuchadnezzar to make known the king's dream along with it's interpretation. The Chaldeans could not do what the king requested of them and they answered him by saying "...there is not a man on earth who could declare the matter for the king..." (Dan.2:10). "Moreover the thing which the king demands is difficult, and there is no one else who could declare it to the king except gods, whose dwelling place is not with mortal flesh (Dan.2:11). These wise men of Babylon were sure nobody could know something that they didn't, but of course as we read further, we see they were entirely wrong. Daniel was able to understand and interpret the kings dream. This example is used 'en passant' to illustrate a similar situation in the world today, where some people, even uninformed christians, are positive no one can know something they don't.

How many times have you heard or said, 'nobody can tell when the Lord is coming, because it is impossible to know, and He even said, "no man knows the day or the hour."? Nearly everyone that has read the Bible or heard anyone preach on bible prophecy is familiar with the concept that Jesus is going to "come like a thief in the night" (1 Thes. 5:2), and that certainly means that you are not going to be aware of anything different when He comes, right? Most people seem to ignore the next few verses, " But you, brethren, are not in darkness, that the day should overtake you like a thief;" (1 Thes. 5:4). This indicates that while some people will be caught off guard, there will be those who are 'in the light' and 'not in darkness' who will be aware of the general time when the Lord will return. In fact the gospel of Luke is firm in an exhortation for the believers to be 'on guard' so that they are not so concerned about everyday life, drunkenness, and the worries of life, that they get caught. But we are to be alert, and prepared so that we may have the strength to escape all these things that are about to take place (Luke 21:34-36). The Word enjoins us to 'ask' about things to come (Isa.45:11), because there are many things that we **can** know about that are going to happen. God has not kept everything a big dark secret, (Isa.45:19), but has revealed many things that are going to take place through the Holy Spirit (Isa.48:16), to His prophets (Amos 3:7). As Christians, we have the Holy Spirit within us who causes us to understand 'spiritually' many things that the natural mind does not know about.

John 16:13

> *But when He, the Spirit of truth, comes, He will guide you into all the truth; for He will not speak on His own initiative, but whatever He hears, He will speak; and He will disclose to you what is to come.*

There are things that are going to take place in the last days that are going to be confusing, disturbing, and misunderstood, but God has seen fit to permit some of His servants to have special insight about His Word, and says "...in the last days. you will clearly understand it." (Jer.23:20). The reference here is in contrast to 'false prophets' who claim to have something from God, but in reality don't. Some of the prophecies are 'sealed' until the time of the end (Dan.12:4,9),when they will be understood by those who 'have insight' (Dan.12:10). God's people will understand "...in the later days you will understand this" (Jer. 30:24), in reference to the wrath of God. In the 'latter days' we will 'clearly understand' the anger of the Lord (Jer. 23:20). There are many things that the Lord is anxious to reveal, but they are not things that He will reveal to us if we don't really care if we know or not. He wants us to respond to Him and inquire about it before He will show us.

Jer. 33:3

> *Call to Me, and I will answer you, and I will tell you great and mighty things, which you do not know.*

The Church and the Tribulation

Nearly everyone is convinced that the world is approaching a cataclysmic event in the very near future, and the overwhelming viewpoint of the majority of Christians is that the Rapture of the Church will precede the seven year tribulation period. Most christians assume that this view is correct for a number of reasons:

1.) The shear volume of pre-tribulational material available as opposed to alternate, equally viable, theological views. As an example, nearly everyone has read "The Late Great Planet Earth", but few have even heard of "The Blessed Hope".

2.) Unrequited trust in the position of eminent preachers, teachers, and professors. Most of us have developed viewpoints of doctrine by virtue of the means by which it arrived rather than our own original research.

3.) Unquestionable devotion to the doctrines and policies of churches and educational institutions that are assumed to be theologically correct. Many people adopt the doctrine taught at particular churches or institutions simply because of a trust in the church or college, and not because they have been proven to be infallible.

4.) An appeal to the human spirit, because it is considered 'spiritual' to be waiting for an 'imminent' return of Christ. Many would be surprised to learn that the term 'waiting' on the Lord really has much more in it than an imminent return.

5.) An appeal to the human soul, because it is logical that Christ would not permit His people to endure punishment along with the judgement of the wicked, therefore He must remove them before the judgement begins.

6.) An appeal to the flesh, because it is not pleasant to look forward to anything that would cause discomfort to our physical bodies. People don't want to hear about any negative aspects of their own life and destiny. I am reminded of my 5 year old daughter that will cover her ears when she is told that she has to do something that she doesn't want to do.
Blocking out the sound does not alter the facts. Christians do not want to hear any other view than the 'fire exit' view, because they think that any other view has to be wrong.

Unfortunately, as much as you may want to believe them, each of these arguments miss the mark in one area or another, and the plain fact of the matter is that the scriptures simply do **not** teach a pre-tribulation rapture.

The Last Trump

2.

A SERPENTINE TRAIL

This chapter is a cursory examination of the Biblical records which reveal that the source of power and authority of the antichrist really originates with Satan himself.

At some specific point in eternity past, God chose to create the heavens and the earth(Gen1:1). Sometime between (Gen.1:1) and the creation of man, God had created Lucifer, as a magnificent, splendid creature who was given a unique position in all of creation. A problem arose when Lucifer, as the anointed cherub, became filled with pride, and desired to have more authority and exercise his will to make himself like the most High God. A confrontation between God and Satan began even before time as we know it began, and has continued throughout the ages. This unusual position of regal authority before God was ultimately reduced to a curse upon the Serpent that Lucifer embodied, and yet his craftiness was still retained (Gen.3). The impressions made on the sands of time by the Serpents prevaricated trail can be found in the pages of Scripture from Genesis to Revelation. He is known by over 30 names in the Scriptures, but his nature remains the same throughout all of time. As an adversary and foe of the Lord God, He is always scheming and deceiving in an attempt to regain his lost position, and if not, to destroy and thwart the purpose and plans of the Almighty as best he can. Satan possessed the Serpent in the Garden of Eden, and interjected doubt as to the Woman's relation to God's Word, then lied to her as to the consequence of disobedience. The graphic temptation was one that affected Body, Soul, and Spirit, (Gen.3:6), just as was the temptation of our Lord (Mat.4). All the kingdoms of the world apparently were within the realm of his dominion (Mt.4:8), and he (Satan), is called 'the god of this world'.

As a liar and the father of lies, he will deceive by causing his people and the whole world (Rev.12:9), to believe what is not true and act in a way that satisfies his own purposes. He was a murderer from the beginning, and people strongly influenced by him, even unknowingly, have a strong propensity toward death, the macabre, have suicidal tendencies, and have little regard for human life.

He has possessed (totally taken control of the physical body, mind and will) of the serpent (Gen 3); Judas Iscariot (Jn 13:2,7; Luke 22:3); and the antichrist. [The inference is made from Rev. 13:2,4,7,14,15.] The power and authority that he has is imparted to the antichrist to enable him to accomplish things humanly impossible to the natural man. He will even seek to simulate the death and resurrection of the Lord, by permitting the man of sin to be killed and then be resurrected.

It was Satan - who was the impetus behind the scene that prompted Herod to attempt to eliminate the Lord at Bethlehem, by having all the male children killed who were under two years old. (Mt.2:16).

It was Satan - who attempted to thwart the Lord's purpose on the cross by causing Peter to try and talk the Lord out of going to Jerusalem (Mt.16:22,23).

It was Satan - that desired to take Peter and sift him as wheat (Lk.22:31).

It was Satan - elevated in pride and authority that was not satisfied, but speaking as the King of Babylon said "I will be like the most high God." (Isa.14).

It was Satan - in whose presence even the spirits of the dead, and all the leaders of the earth who reside in Hell are aroused.

It was Satan - bedecked with jewels, and gold as the anointed cherub, that was filled with unrighteousness, violence and sin. (Ezek.28).

It was Satan - that prophetically is cast to the ground, and whose demise is revealed for all to see as he is turned to ashes and is no more. (Ezek.28).

It was Satan - that sowed the tares, - the children of disobedience in the parable of the sower and the field. (Mt.13).

It was Satan - that originated the rebellion of one third of the angels of heaven who followed him, and caused an angelic battle to occur in heaven with Michael and his angels, and which resulted in banishment from heaven of the evil angels. (Rev.12).

It was Satan - that has blinded the minds of the unbelieving so that the Gospel of Christ is hidden (2Cor.4:3,4).

It was Satan - that Jesus saw falling from heaven as lightening, when the disciples began using the authority Jesus had given them over the enemy.(Lk.10).

IJohn 3:8

> *"...the Son of God appeared for this purpose, that He might destroy the works of the devil."*

It is true that Jesus has given the Church power and authority over the devil, yet even the Archangel Michael was not arrogant but said,'the Lord rebuke you;, and which stands hallmark as an example that the Church should not have a 'cocky' attitude either. The Church often displays ignorance about spiritual warfare by 'chasing the devil' around with about as much effect as an old woman with a broom sweeping the odor of cooking onions out of her kitchen. For some reason we seem to think of the devil as some reversed anthropomorphic irritant that can be simply displaced by loudly addressing him with an emphatic directive, or with some type of incantation. The Hollywood versions of priestly incantations to exorcise Satan's dominion is really a smoke screen to confuse the truth. Talk to a Spirit-filled missionary from Haiti and you will get a totally different concept. My point here, is that while we are being sidetracked by Satan's activities in one area, he is doing the real damage in another. It is like a man fixing a leaking faucet while the whole house is burning down.

We have a record in The Word of some of the ways Satan has attempted (and often succeeded) to hinder the work, effectiveness, and spiritual health of the Church. The following list is not intended to be exhaustive, but only to illustrate some of the different ways Satan has attacked the body of Christ.

a.) a different Gospel (Gal.1:6; Cor.11:4).
b.) false brethren (Gal.2:4).
c.) a spirit of disobedience (Eh.2:2).
d.) another Jesus (2Cor.11:4).
e.) a different spirit (2Cor 11:4).
f.) an angel of light (2Cor.11:14).
g.) false apostles in the Church at Ephesus (Rev.2:2).
h.) false jews of Satan's synagogue, in the Church at Smyrna (Rev.2:9).
i.) Satan even had his own throne in the Church at Pergamum (Rev.2:13).
j.) false prophetess in the church at Thyratira (Rev.2:20)
k.) people that say they are jews and are liars and of Satan's synagogue in the Philadelphia Church.(Rev.2:9).

In fact, the only two churches of Revelation 2,3 that did not have Satan's counterfeits specifically spelled out is Sardis and Laodicea. One apparently was asleep (Rev.3:2), and the other so worldly that they didn't make many waves anyway. I believe there is a direct relationship between the effectiveness of a spirit filled believer (or church) and Satanic opposition. A church or individual that has a close, growing and glowing relationship with the Lord will undoubtedly be challenged in some way. Consider that Jesus went face to face with Satan immediately after a forty day fast (Mt.4).

Satan isn't stupid. He is going to try and stop the effectiveness of the Church any way he can. If I understand the Word of God correctly, the closer we get to the end, the more furious his activity is going to be - until the time of the war with Michael (Rev.12) where Satan is cast down to earth and no longer has access to the throne of God. At that time, he is going to be like a school of unfed Piranhas in a feeding frenzy. Anything even remotely connected with God will be severely persecuted, whether Jew or Gentile, because he knows his time is short. (Rev.12:12).

Another thing that bothers me, is that sometimes we blame the devil for our own sinfulness and wrongdoing. I have even heard nationally known preachers who should know better, make the statement that 'the devil made me do it', when in reality, the sin originated with themselves. One of the keys of repentance is owning up to the responsibility for your own actions. We must 'confess **our** sins' (IJn1:9) for forgiveness, not blame our actions on the devil, even though he may have planted the seed.

Why am I going through all this just to get to the antichrist? Because I believe the Church today is in trouble!!! We have become so worldly and complacent that we couldn't recognize true spiritually if it hit us square in the face. We have progressed to the point that we need a resurrection instead of revival..(pun intended here). If I am correct in my understanding about the Church and the tribulation, we need to be able to recognize the danger signs or we are going to be casualties. How will you know if the Antichrist has come or not? How will you recognize the False Prophet? How will you know the

Lord Jesus when He arrives? If you think of Him as he is often portrayed - as a gentle, long haired, blue eyed, Anglo-Saxon, Tab Hunter type, you may be a candidate for an electro -cardiac shock treatment to get your ticker pumping again.

Suppose for a moment, that we **do** go through the tribulation. (bear with me for a moment, in spite of whatever end time theology you may subscribe to.)

Mat.24:23,24

> *Then if any one says to you,'behold, here is the Christ,' or 'there He is', do not believe him. For false Christs and false prophets will arise and will show great signs and wonders, so as to mislead, if possible, even the elect.*

Mark 13:22

> *For false Christs and false prophets will arise, and will show signs and wonders, in order, if possible, to lead the elect astray.*

Notice that the term is not 'anti-christ', but 'false christ' or pseudo christs. The word literally means "one who in lying fashions, gives himself out to be the Christ, a false messiah"[1] This character is not someone that is the 'opposite 'to Christ but rather one that is 'faking it', and trying to get people to believe that he really is the Christ. The false prophet has a similar definition[2] and is a 'fake'. The problem is that they **will** have the ability to demonstrate supernatural things as evidence to substantiate their claim. Many people will be misled and if possible even the 'elect'. Uh-oh, there's that word again! (**εκλεκτουσ**).

The term is used regarding christians, angels, O.T. Israelites,

---

[1] Arndt & Gingrich, pg. 900.

[2] Ibid. pg.900.

and of the Messiah. It is those whom God has "chosen from the generality of mankind and drawn to himself"[3] Arndt and Gingrich refers specifically to this reference as 'christians'. It is the exact word used in Mt.24:22,31 as well. In verse 31 it speaks about the gathering of the 'elect' from one end of the sky to another. In Rom 8:33, Col.3:12 and Titus 1:1, the Apostle Paul uses the word to describe the Christians. To delineate 'elect' in Mt.24:24 as to pertain to a select company of tribulational jews from the 'elect' of Rev.17:14 as Christians who are "the called and chosen and faithful" goes beyond the scope of Biblical continuity and lexical integrity. Furthermore, it places a burden of proof squarely upon those who would dispensationalize this chapter.

---

[3] Arndt & Gingrich, op.cit. pg.242.

3.

MAN OF SIN

Alias names of Antichrist

In our study on Gog the Dog, I have concluded that the Battle of Gog that is referred to in Ezekiel 38 and 39 is in reality, the Antichrist and all the nations of the world invading the land of Israel at the end of the Tribulation period in a battle better known as Armageddon. The contents of this chapter is a search through the scriptures for more information on that one individual which will more commonly be known as 'The Antichrist'. Surprisingly, there is considerable information available that will reveal many of his 'pseudo' names, country, origin, purpose, number, and relation to prophetic events. We are going to list the references by way of the names that identify him, not necessarily exhaustively, but as many names as we can find.

1.) ***The Man of Lawlessness;***
2 Thes.2:3

> *Let no one in any way deceive you, for it will not come unless the apostasy comes first, and the Man of Lawlessness is revealed, the Son of Destruction*

KJV uses the word 'Sin' to describe this word 'lawlessness',[1] and to be without law is indeed sinful, but 'lawlessness' seems to describe the meaning of this word a little better. This individual will not have any respect for 'queensbury' rules, and he will not honor any code of ethics, morals, or legislated laws. He will make his own laws, which suit his own nefarious motives, and which really originate with Satan himself. Some people thought that Adolf Hitler was the antichrist during World War II, but as atrocious as his acts were, he was not the man. The antichrist will be like him in the sense that he will take the law into his own hands and pronounce judgement upon the Jews, and most likely Christians also.

2.) ***The Son of Destruction;***
KJV uses the word 'perdition'[2] here, but the word literally means '...to destroy utterly; to kill, to bring to nought, make void, to lose, be deprived of, to be destroyed, perish, to be put to death, to die, to be lost, to stray'[3] . The word actually is the same root word as one of the names of Satan, 'Apollyon', and that relates to Antichrist because he will be possessed by Satan, and could be called his son. He will destroy land and people, especially *the* people of *the* land, that is the Jews.

3.) ***That Lawless One;*** 2Thes 2:8;
This verse says that he will be destroyed by the Lord Himself, '...by the appearance of his coming.' This is the second time Paul mentions lawlessness in connection with the Antichrist, and he (antichrist) will no doubt claim just the opposite. He will probably claim to 'establish law and order', just as

---

[1] ***ανομιασ***

[2] ***απωλειασ***

[3] Zondervan lexicon.

Hitler did. If you have ever read any of Hitler's speeches from the days immediately before the Third Reich, you will recognize his line of thinking.

4.) ***The Little Horn;*** Dan.7

This may seem a little strange, but the word 'horn' carries with it a concept of authority, and in this usage, refers to an actual person who gains authority in a kingdom. Unger says, '...they are employed in Scripture as emblems of power'[4] This man of Dan.7 comes up after 10 horns of the 4th beast, and pulls up 3 of the horns by the roots. This strange event is akin to the technique that the Bolsheviks have used to gain power in Russia during the revolution. If someone is in the road to power and authority, he is just eliminated. The word 10 is significant here, and no doubt refers to the same 10 horns of Rev.13:1, which incidently, also has several of the very same beasts named. Many people read Revelation with a desire to understand what is going to happen immediately, without realizing that the language of Revelation, is the symbolism of the O.T. prophecies. You must possess considerable understanding of O.T. prophecies to comprehend the symbolism John is using, and even then it's rough going. Many books have been written about this chapter, and we are going to be quite brief. We believe these first 3 beasts to be Nebuchadnezzar (Babylon), Darius (Media-Persia), Alexander (Macedonia), and Antichrist. This little horn comes up among the 10 horns of the 4th beast, which would be identified by the Roman Empire. Daniel inquired about this vision, and was told that the four beasts were four kings (Dan.7:17). Furthermore, the 4th beast would be a fourth kingdom on the earth, different from the other kingdoms (Dan7:23).

Dan.7:24

As for the ten horns, out of this kingdom ten

---

[4] Unger's Bible Dictionary, page 499.

> *kings will arise; and another will arise after them, and he will be different from the previous ones and will subdue three kings.*

He utters great boasts and wages war with the 'Saints' and overcomes them. the term Saints here, is somewhat subjective, but most likely refers to those Jews that are 'God's people', that is the believing remnant. Antichrist overcomes these Saints and exercises dominion over them for 3 & 1/2 years until the 'ancient of days' comes. His dominion will be judged, removed, annihilated and destroyed forever.

5.) ***A Small Horn ;*** Dan.8;

This is a very important prophetic chapter in the Bible, and reveals some candid things about the end times, and about the Antichrist. Again, Daniel has a vision which has animals in it, but this time, a ram and a male goat are engaged in a battle in which the Ram is butted by the male goat and killed. The male goat had a single 'large horn' that was broken, and out of which came 4 other horns. Out of one of these horns, came forth 'a rather small horn which grew exceedingly great toward the south, toward the east, and toward the Beautiful land.-'(Dan.8:8). The timing of the vision is explained as well as the identity of the 2 animals.

Dan.8:17,19

> *...'Son of man, understand that the vision pertains to the time of the end'. And he said, 'Behold, I am going to let you know what will occur at the final period of the indignation; for it pertains to the appointed time of the end.*

Dan.8:20,21

> *The ram which you saw with the two horns represents the kings of Media and Persia. And the shaggy goat represents the kingdom of Greece, and the large horn that is between his eyes is the first king.*

Now that's pretty explicit. The first king, is undoubtedly,

Alexander the Great, who conquered the Media-Persian empire, and who died rather early in life without any dependents. His kingdom was divided by 4 generals into 4 kingdoms, and out of one of these 4 kingdoms, the little horn comes. It is significant that Antiochus (IV) Epiphanies came from the Selucid dynasty (Syria), since he prefigures the Antichrist more than any other single historical individual, and indeed fulfills much of the prophecy in this chapter. The overall view is 'the time of the end' however, as the context clearly reveals (Dan 8:-17,19).

Causing 'some of the stars' to fall to the earth sounds rather figurative, until the total picture of Revelation 12 is added, where the confrontation between Michael the archangel and the great dragon takes place in heaven, where some of the angels side in with Satan and fall with him (Rev.12:8).

This boastful little horn 'removed the regular sacrifice', and made himself equal with the 'Commander of the host' for three and one half years. At this point there doesn't appear to be a 'regular' sacrifice, and I think this verse should be taken literal.(8:11). He will be insolent, and skilled in intrigue and he will possess great power, but the source of the power is not from himself. He will destroy 'to an extraordinary degree', mighty men and holy people, and he will prosper. He will destroy many 'while they are at ease', and will even oppose the Prince of Princes, then he will be broken without 'human agency'. Antichrist will be thrown into the lake of fire by the Lord at the climax of the battle of armageddon (Rev.19:20), but it is interesting to note that even Antiochus is reputed to have died of worms, his flesh rotting away while he was yet alive, and thus also, 'without human agency'.

Another significant topic of Daniel chapter 8 is the length of time before restoration occurs.

Dan.8:13,14

> *...How long will the vision about the regular sacrifice apply, while the transgression causes*

> *horror, so as to allow both the holy place and the host to be trampled? And he said to me, 'For 2,300 evenings and mornings; then the holy place will be properly restored.*

Obviously, there must be 'the place of His sanctuary', which could be none other than Zion, and also there must be in existence a 'regular sacrifice'. It can pretty well be established that the length of time that the 'saints' will be given into his hand will be 3 1/2 years (Dan.7:25) ie. 'time, times, and half a time', which nearly everyone agrees is the last half of the tribulation, that is, 1260 days. What is the significance of the 2300 days? The key here, must lie in the 'restoration' of the holy place. If the beginning of the time period that is indicated here was the middle of the tribulation, there would remain 1040 days after the tribulation was over before the sacrifice would be restored, which is not comprehensible to me at all, unless we give three years for the Messianic temple to be constructed after the tribulation ends according to the plans given in Ezek. 40. If, however, the 2300 days was from the time the sacrifice was instituted, ie. at the beginning of the tribulation, that is, when the 'firm covenant' for 'one week (7 years) was initiated, then the holy place would be restored 2300 days afterward, or near the end of the great tribulation. As a matter of fact, based on a 360 day year, there would be just about 7 months left before the 7 years would be expired. It seems that everyone has a different concept of when the 7 months of Ezek.39 take place, so here's mine.

Ezek.39:12

> *For seven months the house of Israel will be burying them in order to cleanse the land.*

Three times in five verses, the prophecy refers to 'cleansing' the land. We understand from Deut.21 that dead bodies do defile the land, but there seems to be an emphasis here on cleansing, which I take to mean something special..like, just before the coronation day of the KING. The 7 months are immediately after the 2300 days, and are the last 'cleanup' before the ushering in of the millennial kingdom. This seems to be a plausible alternative, since the arc of the covenant appears in the Lords temple about that time.

Rev. 11:19

And the temple of God which is in heaven was opened; and the ark of His covenant appeared in His temple, and there were flashes of lightening and sounds and peals of thunder and an earthquake and a great hailstorm.

Moreover, this event is concurrent with the seventh trumpet (Rev.11:15). More on this in the trumpet chapter.

6.) ***The PRINCE who is to come.*** (Dan.9)
Dan.9:26,27

Then after the sixty-two weeks the Messiah will be cut off and have nothing, and the people of the prince who is to come will destroy the city and the sanctuary. And its end will come with a flood; even to the end there will be war; desolations are determined.

And he will make a firm covenant with the many for one week, but in the middle of the week he will put a stop to sacrifice and grain offering; and on the wing of abomination will come one who makes desolate, even until a complete destruction, one that is decreed,is poured out on the one who makes desolate.

Many books have been written about Daniel's 70 weeks,[5] and we are making the assumption that the reader is familiar with the term week, meaning 7 years, and for the sake of brevity,

---

[5] see Tatford, *The Climax of the Ages.*

we are not going to lay that foundation again. 'Messiah will be cut off' is referring to that event, when the people of Israel demanded the crucifixion of our Lord, and 'cut Him off' from ushering in the kingdom, nearly 2000 years ago. After that happened, the city was destroyed (70 AD), by Titus the Roman General, who becomes the prefigure of the Antichrist, as the Romans were the 'people of the prince who is to come'. Partly because of this verse, many biblical scholars have concluded that the Antichrist will come from the area of the old Roman Empire, and hence the 10 kingdom federation will be a re-institution of the Roman Empire, since the people that destroyed the city in 70 AD were the Romans.

He (antichrist) will make a firm covenant for seven years, and this covenant will mark the beginning of the 7 year time of unparalleled trouble on the face of the earth, called the Great Tribulation. In the middle of the week, or after 3 and 1/2 years, he (antichrist) will 'put a stop to sacrifice and grain offering'. This undoubtedly refers to 'Jewish' sacrifice and worship, which many believe can't be done until the Jews build a temple in Israel, and re-institute the temple worship that hasn't been done for nearly 2000 years. What constitutes 'sacrifice' may be rather subjective and controversial, but it may be that some kind of worship can be achieved without all the articles of the temple in place. At the very least, it seems that a temple would have to be erected in Jerusalem before this prophecy could be fulfilled. I do not believe that Israel could properly worship God without having the 'Ark of the Covenant' in place, because the Day of Atonement would not have the same significance if the High Priest could not enter the Holy of Holies correctly. This leads me to speculate beyond the scope of prophetic text as to the whereabouts of the Arc of the Covenant, for it is highly possible that it still exists today. It definitely will appear in the heavenly temple (Rev.11:19), but whether it will be discovered before that or not is debatable. It has been missing since 606 BC. when Nebuchadnezzar sacked the temple and took all the valuables to

Babylon. It has been suggested that Jeremiah had the ark removed beforehand, and hidden in some secluded spot. It is this speculation that prompted the filming of one of my favorite movies, 'Raiders of the Lost Arc'.

7.) ***The King of the North*** (Dan.11)

In this amazing chapter, a progression is made from Darius the Mede, to Persia then Greece, which prophetically describes the splitting of Alexander the Great's kingdom into 4 other kingdoms after his four generals; Cassander, Lysimachus, Seleucus, and Ptolemy. This chapter can be seen as historically accurate, by using a history book as a guide, and following each of these individuals as they are mentioned. Dan. 11:15, 'The King of the North will come, cast up a siege mound and capture a well fortified city... '. He will do whatever he wants, and stay for a short time in the 'Beautiful Land' (Palestine). He will come with a proposal of peace, which he will put into effect. While this is probably Antiochus the Great, it is a prefigure of the Antichrist, for he will do similar things. Tatford shows the historical significance of the king of the South as being Egypt, and the king of the north as being Syria.[6] Again, in Dan.11, the antichrist is prefigured by Antiochus IV, who will take the place of the King of the North. Apparently, he isn't in line for the ascension to the throne, but will 'seize the kingdom by intrigue'(Dan.11:21).

Dan.11 reminds me of a script for an allegorical superman movie, where Lex Luthor as the arch enemy of Superman, devises a diabolical scheme to incarcerate Superman while he proceeds to hold some gargantuan weapon that he has gained control over, to ransom the world for an incredible amount of wealth and power. Or perhaps an extremely efficient and shrewd secretary that has taken license with the 'bosses' power, to the point that he usurps the one he is under, without the benefit of an election. I sometimes wondered, for

---

[6] Tatford, *The Climax of the Ages*, p.184

example, when Henry Kissinger was Secretary of State, who was actually piloting the ship.

Dan.11:23

> *And after an alliance is made with him he will practice deception, and he will go up and gain power with a small force of people.*

This may well be the same as the 'firm covenant' of Dan 9:27, as antichrist starts out with a pretty small nation or people, and 'cons' his way into greater power and authority. The Bolshevik revolution started out quite small also, and it may be somewhat akin to Antichrist's rise to power and fame. He uses the time of peace (first 3 1/2 years) to accumulate vast wealth from the 'richest parts of the realm'. He will 'distribute plunder' and 'booty', and devise schemes against strongholds. He has a confrontation with the king of the South..(Egypt), but the Egyptian King experiences an internal revolt that causes his army to disperse, which allows the antichrist to accumulate more wealth. His heart is then turned against the 'holy covenant', which may well be Dan.9:27. He turns a second time against Egypt but shies away because of the 'ships of Kittim'. I could easily visualize a U.S. aircraft carrier in the Mediterranean, issuing an ultimatum here, but of course the scripture doesn't say that.

Dan.11:31

> *And forces from him will arise, desecrate the sanctuary fortress,and do away with the regular sacrifice. And they will set up the abomination of desolation.*

The use of the word 'fortress' is most interesting here, and perhaps says something about the 'temple' of the last time. Certainly, the 'temple' of Herod, that was destroyed by Titus in 70 AD was a veritable fortress that the forces of Israel used it more like an army fort than a site of religious expression.

Dan.11:33

> *And those who have insight among the people will give understanding to the many; yet they will fall by sword and by flame, by captivity and by plunder, for many days.*

Some people are going to understand what the greater picture is, and are going to be teaching the people of Israel, about the time they are going through, and of course about the Lord Jesus, who would make His appearance shortly. Antichrist is going to be a gigantic blasphemer, and speak monstrous things against the 'God of gods', and yet in spite of it, he will prosper remarkably.

Dan.11:37

> *And he will show no regard for the gods of his fathers or for the desire of women, nor will he show regard for any other god; for he will magnify himself above them all.*

The 'gods of his fathers' indicates that he has a religious background, that he doesn't appropriate or respect. An alternate reading here shows 'gods' may be singular, which adds confusion to the matter, for if we could determine that his background was either monotheistic or pantheistic, it could be significant to his identity. He will either be an arrogant male chauvinist, that is cruel to women, or a homosexual. Magnifying himself, indicates that he thinks of himself as possessing some kind of deity, perhaps much the way the early Roman emperors did.

Dan.11:39

> *And he will take action against the strongest of fortresses with the help of a foreign god; he will give great honor to those who acknowledge him, and he will cause them to rule over the many, and will parcel out land for a price.*

He will enlist the help of a 'foreign god', which most likely will be Satanic in origin, but it could also have other bizarre ramifications. After the 1967 war, Israel assumed occupancy of land that Jordan had previously occupied, which was north of Jerusalem, and west of the Jordan, and a little patch of land called the Gaza Strip, where the Philistines once occupied, along the southern coastline. These two areas are of prime concern today, and are territories of much debate between the Israelis, and the Palestinians.(see map 1.). Antichrist will have answers and solutions for some of these 'land' problems, and will solve some of these debates in a unique 'land for bux' deal. Verses 40-43 are significant in that they tell about the nations that Antichrist has confrontations with, and thus rules them out as being the native land that he is from. Among them are Egypt, Syria, Edom, Moab, Ammon, Libya, and Ethiopia.

Dan 11:43

> *But he will gain control over the hidden treasures of gold and silver, and over all the precious things of Egypt;...'*

It has been speculated that 'oil' would be the key to the middle east crises, and the ensuing battleground of Armageddon, and that Russia would be the leader in that struggle. At the present time this seems highly unlikely, because Russia is one of the world leaders in petroleum production. I have read a number of books that make this postulation, but apparently the authors never consulted any factual information in their hypothesis. In 1974 USSR surpassed the U.S. production of oil, and has been gaining ever since. the 1986 Russia produced about 1/5 of the total world production, including the OPEC (arab) nations, which makes it either the largest, or second largest petroleum producer in the entire world. It seems highly unlikely that Russia would go after a nation that doesn't produce very much oil (Israel), for the specific purpose of procuring it. Antichrist may well go after the oil though, since oil would be considered a 'hidden treasure', and to gain control of oil in today's economy would be to possess an enormous leverage in controlling the rest of the world.

He will pitch his tent, or bivouac between Jerusalem and the Mediterranean sea, and he will go forth with a 'great wrath' to destroy and annihilate many people, but rumors from the East and the North will upset him.

8.) ***The King of Babylon*** (Isa.14).

I have included this title because it is a reference directly to Satan's activity prior to the creation of man on the face of the earth. Five times in Isaiah 14, Satan said 'I will'.

I will ascend to heaven
I will raise my throne above the stars of God.
I will sit on the mount of assembly
in the recesses of the north
I will ascend above the heights of the clouds
I will make myself like the Most High.

while The Lord Jesus teaches us to say 'Thy Will be done' in Mat. 6, Satan says 'my will be done'.

Isa.14:16

Those who see you will gaze at you, They will ponder over you, saying,;Is this the man who made the earth tremble, Who shook kingdoms.Who made the world like a wilderness and overthrew its cities, Who did not allow his prisoners to ho home?

This chapter is talking about a MAN, who made the peoples of the world tremble in fear, because he destroyed cities and nations. This is a 'taunt' against the king of Babylon, who was prefigured by Nebuchadnezzar, and who ultimately is possessed by Satan. The prophecy is that Babylon is destroyed and becomes a possession of hedgehogs and swamp water, without offspring and posterity.

An interesting thing about the chapter, is that while the prophecy is directed at the 'King of Babylon', it also calls the land 'Assyria'. Babylon was in Babylonia, not Assyria, so when the prophet uses this terminology, it indicates to me that he is referring to something other than the Babylon of the day, and something other than 'Nebuchadnezzar' the physical king of Babylon.

Isa.14:24,25

The LORD of hosts has sworn saying, 'surely, just as I have intended so it has happened, and just as I have planned so it will stand, to break Assyria in My land, and I will trample him on My mountains. Then his yoke will be removed from them, and his burden removed from their shoulder.

In verse 25, we see 'him' and 'his' refers to the Antichrist who comes from Assyria. 'Them' and 'their' refer to Israel, and the 'I', and 'My' refer to the LORD of hosts, namely the Lord Jesus returning as king of kings and Lord of glory.

9.) ***The Assyrian*** (Isa. 10)

Isa.10:5

Woe to Assyria, the rod of My anger and the staff in whose hands is My indignation,I send it against a godless nation and commission it against the people of My fury to capture booty and to seize plunder, and to trample them down like mud in the streets.

This doesn't sound much like the Lord protecting His people, yet, He has 'chosen' Assyria to be the instrument by which He punishes Israel until they ultimately receive Him as Messiah. When all seems lost, He will return and punish Assyria in 'that day' (Isa.14:20). We know that Assyria did come against Palestine and conquer Israel historically about 701 BC when Hezekiah surrendered Jerusalem to the Assyrian, Sennacherib, but it was only a prefigure of the Antichrist who in 'that day' verse 20, would be destroyed in the midst of the land by the Lord. Because Assyria was not destroyed by the Lord in 701 BC, we look for a later fulfillment of this verse. It is to be noted that some of the bloodiest records of the ancient world are recorded of the Assyrians.

Isa.10:23,24

> *For a complete destruction, one that is decreed, the Lord God of hosts will execute in the midst of the whole land. Therefore thus says the Lord God of hosts, O My people who dwell in Zion, do not fear the Assyrian who strikes you with the rod and lifts up his staff against you, the way Egypt did.*

A complete destruction can be taken to mean several things. Israel is nearly destroyed by the Assyrian, "The rod of my anger...", who acts as the LORDS staff of punishment. Antichrist will then be destroyed by the LORD Himself when his indignation against Israel is complete. The people of Zion are told not to be afraid, even though The Assyrian plunders them, mocks them, is haughty toward them, and destroys them. This chapter is extremely interesting because even the very route that the Antichrist takes in his campaign throughout Palestine is laid out - city by city.

Antichrists very path through the Land is described in detail in verses 28-32. Each of the names mentioned in these verses are names of cities or locations, and a careful observation of the text will let you see the campaign path that Antichrist takes through the Holy land.

Micah 5:5

> *When the Assyrian invades our land, when he tramples on our citadels, then we will raise against him seven shepherds and eight leaders of men.*

In 'that day'(Mic. 5:10), the Lord will deliver a 'remnant of Jacob' from the hand of the Assyrian invader, and execute vengeance in anger and wrath (Mic. 5:15).

Isa.31:8

> *And the Assyrian will fall by a sword not of*

man, and a sword not of man will devour him. So he will not escape the sword,..

The language of this chapter is again, in 'that day', and a day in which the LORD of hosts will come down to wage war on the mountains of Israel. The Assyrian being killed with a sword not of man, is indicative of the fact that the Lord will execute judgement with His sword. This is reflected in Rev.2:12, where Jesus is 'The One who has the sharp two-edged sword', and Rev.19:15, where Jesus has ,'a sharp sword' that comes from His mouth, with which He strikes the nations.

10.) ***Lebanon*** (Isa.10:34)

And Lebanon will fall by the Mighty One.

Lebanon is on the Mediterranean coast, adjacent to Syria, and due north of Israel. Nineveh, the capital city of Assyria, would be about 300 miles east north east of Beirut, so what is the prophet saying anyway? It would seem that if you were to describe the destruction of a nation, you would refer to the capital city in that nation as an illustration of your point, but to also describe the fall of another nation too... there must be a point here that is somewhat esoteric.

The 'mighty one' most likely refers to Messiah when He returns to execute judgement upon the nations, and that is the probable interpretation of this verse.

11.) ***Assyria*** (Isa.30:31)

For at the voice of the LORD Assyria will be terrified, when He strikes with the rod.

The words that accompany the 'rod' are a consuming fire in a cloudburst and downpour of hailstones, and like a torrent of brimstone, which indicate to me that this judgement is against the Antichrist at Armageddon. This is somewhat of a paradox, since the Assyrians were very cruel and ferocious in war. They were stern disciplinarians, and were intense and intolerant where religion was concerned. "Like the Ottoman Turks they formed a military state, at the head of which was a king, who was both leader in war and chief priest,..."[7] In that respect they were different from the Babylonians, because the Babylonians held to a theocratic state. The Assyrians conscripted every male into the large standing army, and also incorporated mercenaries, who received 'booty' from the captured states. Constant war was necessary to maintain the large force of soldiers, who demanded payment in booty of the captured lands. The antichrist will also 'give great honor to those who acknowledge him, and will cause them to rule over the many,...' (Dan.11:39).

The second empire of Assyria was begun by Tiglath-pileser IV (745-727 BC), and was reorganized into a two fold policy; "...to weld western Asia into a single empire, held together by military force and fiscal laws, and to secure the trade of the world for the merchants of Nineveh "[8]. Antichrist will 'honor the god of fortresses', and will utilize warfare and war techniques to his own end, and he will gain control over 'the hidden treasures of gold and silver...' and amass great wealth.(Dan.11). Under Essar-haddon, the second empire of Assyria reached its peak of power and prosperity, even having Babylon as a second capital to Nineveh. The two city states of Babylon and Nineveh are near each other, and were related by similar language and bloodlines. When Assyria fell, the Neo-Babylonian empire began as the dawn of a new era, and assumed control of the land that Assyria once held.

12.) ***The King of Assyria*** (Isa.37:4,6,7)

> *...Behold, I will put a spirit in him so that he shall hear a rumor and return to his own land. And I will make him fall by the sword in his own land.*

This section dealing with Hezekiah, obviously is speaking

---

[7] I.S.B.E. vol.I pg.291

[8] ISBE Vol.I, pg. 294.

about Sennacherib, the king of Assyria, but this verse 7 that we quoted, seems to be out of context with the 701 BC invasion of Jerusalem by the Assyrian. It pertains rather, to a future generation at the time of the end, when the Assyrian will indeed, fall by the hand of the Lord. But, his own land? II Kings 19:37 tell us that Sennacherib returned to Nineveh, and was killed with the sword by his two sons Adrammelech and Sharezer while he was worshiping in the house of his god. This is repeated in Isa.37:38, and probably shouldn't be included here, except for the fact that verse 36 says that the angel of the LORD went out, and struck 185,000 in the camp of the Assyrians, which emphasizes the typeology of Antichrist.

Nahum 3:18

> *Your shepherds are sleeping, O king of Assyrian your nobles are lying down. Your people are scattered on the mountains, and there is no one to regather them.*

This doesn't seem like a title of Antichrist at all, until one sees the picture of the entire book of Nahum, which in itself is an 'oracle of Nineveh', (see item 21).

13.) ***A Destroyer*** (Jer.4:7)

> *A lion has gone up from his thicket, and a destroyer of nations has set out; He has gone out from his place to make your land a waste. Your cities will be ruins without inhabitant.*

This is a besieger from a far country, from the north, who brings great destruction, in 'that day'. Disaster upon disaster is proclaimed, and the whole land is devastated. This destroyer is the agency of the "fierce anger of the LORD" who will destroy greatly, yet the Lord says that he will not execute a complete destruction.

14.) ***The Destroyer*** (Jer.6:26)

> *...for suddenly the destroyer will come upon us.*

A great nation from the land of the north, that are a cruel and ride on horses. The false prophets pacify the people and heal their wound slightly, saying 'peace, peace', when there is no peace. Just when the people are beginning to think of peace and safety, the destroyer attacks, but only for a short while, and then he also is destroyed by the LORD.

(Jer.48:32)

...The destroyer has fallen.

Chapter 48 of Jeremiah deals with the fall of Moab, which is directly south of Israel, on the eastern side of the Dead Sea. It is known as Jordan today, and will be all but destroyed by the Lord, when He comes to deliver Israel from the hands of the Antichrist at the last great campaign of the battle of Armageddon. (48:1)'...Woe to Nebo, for it has been destroyed'. (48:9)'...And her cities will become a desolation, without inhabitants in them.'

15.) ***The Horn of Moab*** (Jer.48)

Jer.48:25

The horn of Moab has been cut off, and his arm broken, declares the LORD.

'The disaster of Moab will soon come,...'(Jer.48:16). It has been put to shame (48:20), and destroyed, and will become a laughingstock, and an object of terror to all around him (48:39-), and Moab will be destroyed from being a people(48:42). Yet the mercy of God triumphs over destruction, for He will restore the fortunes of Moab in the 'latter days'(48:47). Moab was the son of Lot through his daughter, which makes him somewhat of a cousin to Abraham, and 'Semitic'. There is a considerable volume of prophecy given to the destruction of Moab and Edom, which may be significant in itself.

16.) ***The Hammer of the Whole Earth*** (Jer.50:23)

How the hammer of the whole earth has been cut off and broken! How Babylon has become an object of horror among the nations!

This title has an almost humorous 'ring' to it, that reminds me of Saturday Night Wresting. It is not really humorous though, because the Antichrist becomes the agency with which the Lord punishes all the peoples of the world, and especially Israel (51:20), yet He say '...You are My war-club, My weapon of war;' which could also apply to 'Jacob' (51:19). More likely, it is the reference made to Babylon of the last days, and with which the Lord will shatter nations, destroy kingdoms, shatter horse and rider, chariots and rider, man and woman, old man and youth, young man and virgin, shepherd and flock, farmer and team, governors and prefects. In the end Babylon will be a desolation forever, and without inhabitant (51:26,29) when the Lord executes His vengeance (51:6,11). Nebuchadnezzar's Babylon of the Chaldeans, was to be destroyed by the 'destroyers' from the north. It did indeed become a heap of ruins without inhabitant, and a haunt of jackals, as history and archaeology attest. There are other 'long range' prophecies concerning Babylon which could only be fulfilled at the time of the very end.

17.) ***The King of Babylon*** (Ezek.32).

Ezek.32:11

For thus says the Lord God, The sword of the king of Babylon shall come upon you.

For the most part, chapter 32 deals with a lamentation over Pharaoh king of Egypt, who will be destroyed by the king of Babylon who will be God's 'war club' and cause Egypt to be a 'desolation'(32:15), when 'I smite all those who live in it, then they shall know that I am the LORD.' (32:15).

18.) ***Gog*** (Ezek.38,39).

The problem with Ezek.38,39, is that we have taken it out of context from the rest of prophetic scriptures, and have made a doctrine out of somewhat subjective material. When taken in the context of the whole of Biblical prophecy, Gog can be no other than the Antichrist of the last days of the great tribulation, as we have discussed to some length in the chapter 'Gog the Dog'.

19.) ***The Northern Army*** (Joel 2)

Much of the language of Joel is highly allegorical and metaphorical in its relation to the end times and the conditions at the very end. The norther army, is a tool with which the Lord chastens all nations, especially Israel. It is also referred to as 'His army',(2:11), and 'My great army' (2:25), which 'I',(Jehovah), sent among them. I think one of the keys to understanding the prophecies of the last times, is in the mercy of the Lord, for He is always desirous of repentance and faith. In this chapter of Joel, that deals with 'darkness and gloom', a 'day of clouds and thick darkness', fire, flames, and fear, when 'all faces turn pale', astronomical changes that affect the sun and the moon, earthquakes, and trembling of the heavens, yet the mercy of the Almighty still shows through.

Joel 2:12,13

> *Yet even now, declares the LORD, return to Me with all your heart, and with fasting, weeping, and mourning; and rend your heart and not your garments; Now return to the LORD your God, for He is gracious and compassionate, Slow to anger, abounding in lovingkindness and relenting of evil.*

Who knows whether the Lord will show mercy or not if one should repent in the midst of destruction? I believe that we have become so antiseptic as christians in this age that we are ready to call down the thunder and lightening on the enemies of the Lord, without any display of compassion for the lost souls of those who are 'without'. Even in the midst of judgement we see the mercy of the Lord.

Joel 2:32

> *And it will come about that whoever calls on the name of the LORD will be delivered; For on Mount Zion and in Jerusalem there will be those who*

> *escape, as the LORD has said, even among the survivors whom the LORD calls.*

20.) ***A Wicked Counselor*** (Nahum 1)
The Lord 'is slow to anger and great in power', yet He reserves vengeance and great wrath for His adversaries. In this 'oracle' of Nineveh, where His wrath is 'poured out like fire'. The 'wicked counselor' has 'plotted evil' against the Lord (1:11), and the Lord will break 'his' yoke bar from Israel, and tear off his shackles.

21.) ***The Wicked One*** (Nahum 1)
This 'wicked one' from Nineveh, will never again pass through Israel, for he will be cut off completely (1:15). Again, we see the mercy of God showing through the judgement;

Nah.1:15

> *Behold on the mountains the feet of him who brin[gs] good news, who announces peace!...*

22.) ***The One who Scatters*** (Nahum 2)
Verses 2:3,4 could easily be construed to be interpreted as a tank invasion into the land of Palestine. The chariots are enveloped in 'flashing steel', and brandish cypress spears (front cannons). They dash to and fro like 'lightening flashes', and rush wildly in the squares and madly in the streets. He (Antichrist) plunders silver, gold and wealth from every kind of desirable object (2:9), and with desolation and waste causes fear that makes hearts melt and knees to knock (2:10). But the Lord of hosts has his own anti-chariot weapons, for He says,'...I will burn up her chariots in smoke,...'(2:13).

23.) ***Antichrist*** (I John 2)
I Jn.2:18

> *Children, it is the last hour; and just as you heard that antichrist is coming, even now many antichrists have arisen; from this we know that it is the last hour.*

I Jn.2:22

Who is the liar but the one who denies that Jesus is the Christ; This is the antichrist, the one who denies the Father and the Son.

I Jn.4:3

and every spirit that does not confess Jesus is not from God; and this is the spirit of the anti-christ, of which you have heard that it is coming, and now it is already in the world.

24.) ***The Beast Coming out of the Sea*** (Rev.13:1)

And he stood on the sand of the seashore; And I saw a beast coming up out of the sea, having ten horns and seven heads, and on his horns were ten diadems, and on his heads were blasphemous names.

I could wish that the Apostle John would have given us a few more specifics regarding the term 'beast', because there are so many prophetic beings that are just called 'beast' that it gets extremely confusing, but perhaps that may be intentional. While the language is highly figurative and related to the illustrations of the Old Testament, particularly of Daniel, it technically, represents a ten kingdom empire that emerges from among the masses of the populace in the last days. It has components from different animals, which themselves represent national strengths and weaknesses, and which, when combined, create a real monster. I identify the antichrist with the 'beast coming out of the sea', because 'he' speaks blasphemies (13:5), and that seems more appropriately done by a person than a nation. Many Biblical scholars of times past have come up with all kinds of novel ideas regarding this beast, not a few of which identify it as a revived Roman Empire, Russia and its satellites, The Roman Catholic Church, and probably the most popular, the European Common Market.

Satan is 'the dragon' that gives antichrist the power and authority to elevate himself to a position of deity. One of the beast's heads is wounded fatally and was healed, which I believe to be the resurrection of the antichrist, since (Rev.13:-12) says that the first beast had a fatal wound that was healed, and (Rev.13:14) says that he had a sword wound and came back to life. He has tremendous military power because people say 'who is able to wage war with him?'(Rev.13:4). He is given authority to act for 42 months or 3 & 1/2 years, and make war with the saints and overcome them. The use of the word 'saints' is probably to be understood in terms of what we have already established saints as being, namely, the believing remnant of Israel that shall be saved at the time of the end. (Rev.13:7) by itself, would not be sufficient to make that conclusion, but in addition to the rest of the prophecies in the O.T. the identity seems quite conclusive. All of the people of the earth will worship him, and that is qualified by the statement of those '...whose name has not been written from the foundation of the world in the book of life of the lamb..' (Rev.13:8).

The term 'beast coming up out of the earth' refers to another individual which could be compared to a general or religious secretary of state for the first beast, and is commonly referred to as the 'false prophet'. Many people think that the false prophet is 'jewish' while the antichrist is 'gentile', but some of these concepts are based more on imagination than substance.

25.) ***666*** (Rev.13:18)

> *Here is wisdom. Let him who has understanding calculate the number of the beast, for the number is that of a man; and his number is six hundred and sixty-six.*

This enigmatic number has intrigued Bible scholars since the time it was written. There have been theories upon theories by many different students from different ages, different countries, and different theological persuasions. The number 6 is[9] 'hex', which in today's computer language, is an abbreviated form of 'hexadecimal' and means a base of 16. I doubt that 'hex' has any significance here, but it should be noted anyway. The word for 'calculate' is also an interesting word[10] and it comes form a word which means pebble, and hence to 'compute, reckon, calculate'[11], as one might do with an abacus. The verse is clearly saying that there is some calculating to do to determine the number from the name. The question is 'what is the mechanism used to calculate the number from the name?' The KJV makes things extra difficult by adding the old English means of stating numbers, which is so antiquated that you have to decipher the English before you figure out what the 'number' is to start with. Incidently some old manuscripts have the number 616 rather than 666, so if you are familiar with the apparatus of variant readings of the 'Textus Receptus', you may want to investigate this further. I have used numerous techniques to decipher this enigmatic segment, but I believe the solution is not really as complex as one might imagine. The means of counting in the Roman world at the time Revelation was written was by Roman Numerals, and it is my feeling, that they are the key to understanding the cryptology. Since a greek (or latin) letter also doubles as a numeral, it seems to be a logical explanation, especially when you consider that placing the numerals in ascending order (right to left) { DCLXVI } adds up to 666. Just in case you are a little rusty on your roman math, it is 1 + 5 + 10 + 50 + 100 + 500 = 666. I believe that antichrist will have these six letters in his name, and that will help to identify him. For example, the name will have many other letters in it that aren't significant, since we only add

---

[9] (εξ)

[10] (ψρφισατω)

[11] Bagster's Lexicon.

any of these six that we find. A hypothetical name such as [A**L**e**X**an**D**er **C**o**V**ertrush**I**nsky], for example contains these six numerals, and could be added up to 666. Even if someone politically active has these numerals in his name does not necessarily make him antichrist however, since he must also fit into the framework that we have uncovered from our investigation of the scriptures.

He makes some kind of rule, that you must have a mark on your forehead or your right hand, either the name or number of the beast before you are able to buy or sell. A christian or redeemed remnant jew will have a difficult time if he is caught in this dilemma, because if he doesn't worship the image of the beast (Rev.13:15) he will be killed, and if he receives the mark of the beast in order to buy or sell, he will also receive the wrath of the God (Rev.14:9,10). Talk about being between a rock and a hard place..oi vey'. I think that this is the kind of decision that will unequivocally sort the wheat from the tares, the genuine christian that possesses the Holy Spirit from those that may be outstanding church-going people who have never made a personal commitment to the Lord. This book is not an evangelistic book, but - If you have enough interest in this subject to read this far, you owe it to yourself to make sure that you are on the right side when the chips fall. Ask God to show you what to do; start reading the Gospel of John; and find some Christian that can help you get started.

A BRIEF SUMMARY

This section is a condensed compendium that includes some of the material we have covered in the names of antichrist, and some specifics about his nature, background, authority, idiosyncracies and characteristics by which we may be better able to identify this 'the man of sin' when he appears. Some of the material cited is admittedly subjective, and some prophecies have already seen one or more near view fulfillments.

Man of sin

1.) He is called a 'foolish' and 'worthless' shepherd (Zech.11:16,17). The word 'shepherd' normally indicates responsibility for people, and usually 'God's people' are called 'sheep'. This man has responsibility for people, perhaps both spiritually and politically, and doesn't do a very good job taking care of them.2.)

2.) He will have a sword wound on his arm and right eye (Zech.11:17). The use of the word 'sword' most likely indicates that he bears the scars of an old war wound, which might not necessarily mean he was struck with a steel blade, but that he incurred a serious wound.

3.) His arm will be totally withered (Zech.11:17), which will be very obvious to his physical appearance, and will be the result of the battle wound.

4.) His right eye will be blind (Zech.11:17). This might not be a noticeable defect, such as the late Moshe Dayan who wore a patch over one eye.

5.) He receives a fatal sword wound and is resurrected (Rev.13:14). This is the 'fatal wound' of Rev.13:3,12 that was miraculously healed. It is thought by many scholars that it is this wound, death, and resurrection by which the Antichrist emulates the death, burial and resurrection of the Lord. The scripture doesn't indicate that this is 'faked', but that he really does die and come back to life. Perhaps it is at this juncture that Satan personally indwells his being.

6.) His resurrection attracts a large following (Rev.13:3). People are always attracted to things that happen in a 'supernatural' realm. I am always amazed that charlatans can attract such large crowds with slight of hand chicanery, while a down and out person whose life is totally transformed by the salvation of the Lord, receives such little attention. People are going to be aware that he experiences a supernatural resuscitation to life, and are going to be attracted to him for that reason.

7.) He will come from the area of the old Greek empire (Zech.9:13) and also (Joel 3:6), where the translation 'Greeks' comes from a literal translation 'sons of Javan'. Javan was the name given to Greece by the Hebrews, but more accurately refers to the Ionians who inhabited the coasts of Lydia and Caria.[12] Ancient Lydia was in Asia Minor and would be within the modern nation of Turkey, adjacent to the Aegean Sea. A third explanation, is that 'Greeks' refer to 'Gentiles', as is often the case with the KJV in the NT. A fourth and more probable explanation, is that Greeks refers to the great world kingdom of Alexander the Great, whose kingdom was divided into four parts. The northern kingdom which was ruled by Alexander's general Seleucus, was the area of Syria, and from which the 'little horn' (Antiochus Epiphanies IV) of Daniel 8:9 came.

8.) He is given authority for 42 months to utter blasphemies (Rev.13:5). The prophets use several different means to indicate a time period, which is to confirm the meaning of the time. Here 42 months is used to indicate a 3 1/2 year period of time in which the antichrist acts arrogantly against God, and speaks out against the Lord.

9.) He makes war with the saints (Israel) and overcomes them and exerts authority over every tribe, people, and tongue (Rev.13:7). Not only does he become a force in the middle east, but everyone else in the world is sub-

---

[12] *Ungers Bible Dictionary*, pg.556

ject to his authority also.

10.) All the people of the earth will worship him, except those whose names are in the book of life (Rev.13:8).

11.) He blasphemes God, His name, His tabernacle and those who dwell in heaven (Rev.13:5).

12.) He climbs to power by uprooting 3 other kings (Dan.7:8). He 'pulls them out by the roots', which implies that he doesn't leave any room for heirs of the 3 kings to rise to power. Perhaps he commits genocide on them along with their families.

13.) He will intend to make alterations in times and law (Dan7:25). His system of law (justice?) is tied in with the calender. It would not surprise me to find out that this is referring to a caliph who will institute a mandatory month of ramadan and institute changes in moral laws to a reflect a 7th century Koran.

14.) Saints will be given into his hand for 3 1/2 years (Dan.7:25). I believe these 'saints' are not 'angels', but the redeemed of Israel.

15.) His kingdom will be annihilated and destroyed forever (Dan.7:26). I don't think this comes as any surprise to even a cursory student of the Bible.

16.) He is skilled in intrigue (Dan.8:23). He will be 'hard headed' and insolent, and will have the tongue of a politician to speak lies with a straight face. Covert operations will be the order of the day for his administration.

17.) He will magnify himself (Dan.8:25). He will be an egotist of humongous proportions, and like the Caesars of Rome, become so self centered that he thinks of himself as a god to be worshipped.

18.) He will oppose the Prince of princes (the LORD) (Dan.8:-25).

19.) He will be broken without human agency (Dan.8:25). The LORD is personally going to execute judgement against him.

20.) He will make a 7 year covenant with Israel (Dan 9:27). This is the clear indicator of the identity of antichrist to the believers who are watching the international situation. A seven year peace agreement will be achieved, and signed by the antichrist and Israel. I visualize this to be similar to the agreement that Israel and Egypt signed on March 26. 1979.

21.) He will put a stop to the sacrifice and grain offering after 3 1/2 years (Dan 9:27),(Dan.11:31). The 7 year peace plan only lasts for 3 1/2 years and then antichrist stops the sacrifice and grain offering. The initial peace plan may not have specifically involved the temple worship, but something happens that arouses the ire of antichrist, and he takes drastic action against this sacrifice.

22.) He will commit the 'Abomination of Desolation' (Dan.-9:27) (Dan.11:31). {see the chapter on this for more information}

23.) He speaks monstrous things against God (Dan11:36). This is not an every day curse against God, but there is something extraordinary in the blasphemy of this person.

24.) He will prosper (Dan 11:36). In spite of all the blasphemy, and terrible things that he does, he is going to be successful in the programs that he initiates.

25.) He will show no regard for the gods of his fathers (Dan.11:37). The use of the plural in 'gods' indicates that he will not be from a monotheistic origin, and the plural of 'father' indicates that his nationality has a long historical past.

26.) He shows no regard for the desire of women (Dan.11:37). Either he is a male chauvinist, or a homosexual.

27.) He will honor the god of fortresses Dan 11:38 which his fathers did not know. He will disregard this national legacy, and adopt a new and 'foreign' god, of force who will help him against the 'strongest of fortresses'. If this fortress is spiritual in nature, it would most likely be 'the kingdom of God', and if it is political in nature, it would most likely be 'The United States' or whatever nation is the superpower at that particular time. It is clear from Revelation 12, that there will be a 'spiritual' war in heaven at the time of the end, and it is also clear from Revelation 13 that antichrist will make war with the 'saints' and overcome them. Incidently, the word 'Kremlin' apparently means 'fortress'..hmmm.

28.) He honors his god with gold, silver, costly stones, and treasures (Dan.11:38), and he seems to have plenty of money.

29.) He will take action against the strongest of fortresses with the help of a 'foreign god' (Dan.11:39). We will understand more clearly what is meant by this verse as we approach the time of the end.

30.) He will give great honor to those that acknowledge him (Dan.11:39).

31.) He parcels out land for a price (Dan 11:39). He has the solutions to the land problems in the middle east, and solves the problem by parcelling out and selling real estate in what I call the 'land for bux' scam.

32.) He is NOT from Egypt or Syria because he will have confrontations with each of them (Dan.11:40).

33.) He is NOT from Edom, Moab, or Ammon, because these are rescued out of his hand (Dan.11:41). These countries are the present nation of Jordan.

34.) He will gain control over the hidden treasures of gold and silver and over the precious things of Egypt.(Dan.11-:43).

35.) Libya and Ethiopia will follow at his heals (Dan.11:43), which indicates he will NOT be from either of these nations, but perhaps they will follow him like a dog follows his master.

36.) He will be a moslem (Isa.41:25). I realize this is rather subjective, but what other religion calls on the name of God at daybreak? Moslems are required to pray 5 times per day.

37.) He will come from the kingdom of the North.(Jer.50:3, 6:22). The near view on the prophecies about the invasion of the king of the north pertains to the invasion of Assyria into Israel, and Babylon into Judah. The same prophecies also reflect a far view because of their relationship to the 'day of the LORD', the judgement of antichrist, and the revival of spiritual Israel.

38.) He is going to turn against Egypt and almost totally destroy her (Ezek.30:25, Dan.11:25). On first glance these scriptures seem unrelated, since one declares Babylon will invade Egypt and the other declares that the king of the north (Syria) will invade Egypt. Moreover, the near view has long since been fulfilled (over 2000 years ago), but in one case we see the 'abomination of desolation' following, and in the second it states that "...then they will know that I am the LORD". Since both of these prophecies will be fulfilled in or after the tribulation period, we conclude that the antichrist will indeed invade Egypt. Egypt's destruction and demise will ultimately be left to Israel, however, as we discover in another chapter.

39.) He is going to be proficient in the use of terrorism (Ezek.32:23).

40.) He will return to his own land and be killed there by the Lord.(Isa.37:4,6,7). The near view was fulfilled by Sennacherib, the Assyrian king, who returns to his homeland as a result of a rumor, and who dies at the hands of his own sons.

41.) He will dupe Jordan into helping him by having them betray Israel (Ezek.35:5). The reason for this speculation, is that Mt. Seir (Jordan) delivers the sons of Israel to the power of the sword at the 'time of their calamity', and their destruction will come by the hands of the Antichrist, not the hands of Mt. Seir. The time of their calamity is demonstrably the culmination of the great tribulation, and is further emphasized by the specific language, "...at the time of the punishment of the end...".

42.) He invades the land of Israel and tramples citadels and territory (Micah 5:5,6).

43.) The probability is that his ancestry is Hametic because of the relationship with the 'land of Nimrod' (Micah 5:6).

44.) He will encourage people to forsake the holy covenant by smooth words (Dan.11:30).

45.) He will use 'smooth words' to cause those who act 'wickedly' toward Israel to become polluted by godlessness (Dan.11:32).

46.) The color of the uniforms of his army is 'scarlet' (Nahum 2:3).

47.) The emblems or shields of antichrists mighty men are red in color (Nahum 2:3).

48.) Antichrist will be subject to rumors, especially from the east and the north (Dan.11:44).

49.) He sets up his royal camp between the Mediterranean and Jerusalem (Dan.11:45).

50.) There is something 'royal' about him, because his camp is called a 'royal pavilion' (Dan.11:45).

51.) He is called a king (Dan.11:36).

52.) He seizes his kingdom by intrigue, and gets power that wasn't conferred on him (Dan.11:21).

53.) He comes into power in a time of peace and tranquility, even though it is a brief and false peace (Dan.11:21).

54.) He is able to shatter strong military forces that oppose him (Dan.11:22).

55.) He comes into power with only a small force behind him (Dan.11:23).

56.) He speaks lies around a table (Dan.11:27).

57.) He gives special honors to those who defect from Israel (Dan.11:30).

58.) He comes from the Old Roman Empire, though he is not necessarily Roman or Italian (Dan.9:26). The reason for this is that 'the people of the prince' are the ones that already have destroyed the temple, and that was the Romans in 70 AD. The verse is worded like a riddle, and could be many things, perhaps even pertaining to the Idumeans who were in Jerusalem causing havoc and destruction at the time when Rome destroyed the temple. Another consideration is that Rome often employed mercenaries as warriors in their armies, so the term in the verse 'the people' might apply to them. This verse, though enigmatic, has caused many to conclude conclusively that the 'common market' nations are the present kingdom of the antichrist, because they are included in the boundary of the old Roman Empire, and because there are a specific number of nations involved. If the common market nations are the kingdom of the antichrist, it would seem that there would have to be 13 nations at the present time, since antichrist uproots 3 of them. Who, after all, did destroy the temple?

59.) He is referred to as 'the hammer of the whole earth' (Jer.50:23), which indicates that he is powerful enough to 'beat up' any nation that opposes him.

60.) The Lord will trample him on the mountains of Israel (Isa.14:25).

61.) Antichrist's nation is an ancient, enduring nation with a language that the Jews don't understand (Jer.5:15). The near view of this prophecy pertained to Babylon. (see map #3 on the ancient boundary of The Assyria Empire).

62.) He will come into possession of a great army with much equipment and weapons of warfare. (Dan.11:13).

63.) He has a task force of tanks (Nahum 2:3,4). How would you describe a 20th century tank if you lived in 700 BC?

4.

GOG the DOG

Who the heck is Gog?

If I asked the question, 'Have you ever heard of the term Gog?', some of you would be totally blank, assuming that I misspelled the word, while others, who are keeping abreast of Biblical prophecy, and have read a few of the current prophetic books on the market, will undoubtedly say...SURE! It comes from Ezekiel 38 and 39, and it is the leader of the Russian hordes that invade the land of Israel sometime before the rapture of the church, and he meets his untimely demise with only a portion of his army left standing. This at least, is a concept that I have had for a number of years, that I would like to pursue a little further. You may be surprised to learn that there is more to be said about 'Gog' in the scripture than just Ezekiel, although that's the key scripture that records his exploits. First of all, we want to examine the origin of this individual from the scriptures, and then see if any information can be found from other sources to verify the claims.

Genesis 10:1-5;

> *Now these are the records of the generations of SHEM, HAM, and JAPHETH, the sons of NOAH; and sons were born to them after the flood. The sons of Japheth were GOMER and MAGOG and Madai*

and Javan and TUBAL and MESHECH and Tiras. And the sons of GOMER were Ashkenaz and Riphath and TOGARMAH. And the sons of Javan were Elishah and TARSHISH, Kittim and Dodanim. From these the coastlands of the nations were separated into their lands, every one according to his language, according to their families, into their nations.

The capital letters are mine, to emphasize the names that occur in Ezekiel. This whole chapter in Genesis is devoted to the Ancestral history of the people after the flood. The thing that I want to emphasize here is that all the names that are associated with Ezekiel, that are mentioned in Genesis 10, proceed from Japheth, and are what we would consider 'gentiles'. The Semitic people came from Shem, and the Hametic people from Ham. An interesting thing to note, is that Ham is usually associated with Africa, and the black race, but this is not so. The sons of Ham were the progenitors of the Babylonians, Assyrians, as well as a lot of the 'ites' of the land of Canaan, that Israel had serious dealings with when they entered the promised land. It is a common misconception that the Middle East is a turmoil of Semitic origin. Some of the Arabic peoples do come from the sons of Shem, but some, such as Iran, are quite explicit about the fact that they are NOT Semitic. I think this has a substantial bearing on the understanding of the whole problem in the Middle East today.

Chapter 1 of I Chronicles also gives a similar genealogical history of the progeny of the sons of Noah, which we are not going to repeat, with the exception of an interesting thing in chapter 5.

I Chronicles 5:1-4;

Now the sons of Reuben the first-born of Israel (for he was the first-born, but because he defiled his father's bed, his birthright was given to the sons of Joseph the son of Israel; so that he is not

> *enrolled in the genealogy according to the birthright. Though Judah prevailed over his brothers, and from him came the leader, yet the birthright belonged to Joseph), the sons of Reuben the first-born of Israel were Hanoch and Pallu, Hezron and Carmi. The sons of Joel were Shemaiah his son, GOG his son, Shimei his son,..*

This is the only reference I can find to the Biblical account of where Gog came from, but isn't it interesting, that it is the *only* name in the list that isn't from the sons of Japheth, and that this one is of 'Jewish' origin? This is conjecture at this point, but...is it possible that the last great charge against the Israel, who are dwelling in the land, would be led by one of their own people? There is more to be said about this later on.

I want to list some of the thoughts that the historians and scholars have written about Gog, and see if there is any unanimity of scholarship. One of my favorite Bible dictionaries has this to say:

> "Ezekiel 38,39 which deal with Gog,the prince,and Magog, his land, describe the actual invasion of Palestine by a great northern confederacy, ostensibly headed up by Russia...and evidently precedes the actual battle of Armageddon by a number of years."[1]

Dr. Unger seems to be a bit more speculative in these statements than I feel is warranted by the scriptural information available. If there is substantive evidence that Russia is indeed equivalent with Gog, then that reference should have been stated, as well as the evidence to support the invasion preceding the battle of Armageddon. Speculation such as described

---

[1] Merrill F. Unger, *Unger's Bible Dictionary*,(1961), pg.418

by the eminent Dr. can only lead to erroneous conclusions by others that rely on his usual 'pure' scholarship. Reeve makes a rather astounding statement about Gog as well, when commenting about Ezekiel, and the invasion of Gog into the land of Palestine:

> "The fulfillment of this strange prophecy can never be literal".[2]

Today, a statement such as this seems totally out of order, but at the time it was written, it *was* impossible, since Israel wasn't even a nation, and the rest of the confederacy were not in view either. The historian Josephus has a few things to say about some of these names;

> "..for Gomer founded those whom the Greeks now call Galatians, [Galls,] but were then called Gomerites. Magog founded those that from him were named Magogites, but who are by the Greeks called Scythians. Now as to Javan and Madai, the sons of Japhet; from Madai came the Madeans, who are called Medes by the Greeks; but from Javan, Ionia and all the Grecians are derived. Thobel founded the Thobelites, who are now called Iberes; and the Mosocheni were founded my Mosoch; now they are Cappadocians."[3]

> "Phut also was the founder of Libyia, and called the inhabitants Phutites, from himself, for of the four sons of Ham, time has not at all hurt the name of Chus; for the Ethiopians, over whom he reigned, are even at this day, both by themselves and by all men in Asia, called Chusites."[4]

I have included these quotes from Josephus, because I don't

---

2 J.J. Reeves, *I.S.B.E.* vol II, pg.1273.

3 Josephus, *Antiquities of the Jews*, book 1, ch.VI, pg.30.

4 Josephus, op.cit.

believe most readers will have access to that book to research for themselves. Chus and Phut are Cush and Put in Ezek.38:5, and along with Persia.[modern Iran], represent an Arab alliance with the Japhathites or [non-Semetics]. In short, the Jewish nation in this chapter doesn't have many friends!

If Josephus is correct, we can draw some interesting observations from these quotations. The array of nations against Israel in the last days are specifically named, and if we can relate the ancient name for the modern countries, we may be able to see history in the making before our very eyes. I have always associated 'Gomer' with modern Germany (I'm not even sure why), but according to Josephus, it may well be part of the area now occupied by modern Turkey. Magog is related to the ancient Scythians, and may well be the reference to the modern nation of Russia, since the nation is thought to come from an area north of the Black and Caspian Seas. It is easy to over generalize some of these ancient nations, and make firm conclusions that the entire nation of modern Russia is meant, when in fact, it may not represent the conglomerate of modern Soviet states at all, but only a southern state. Another confusing name is 'Mesech' from which many prophecy scholars get modern 'Moscow'. It is interesting to note that Josephus relates it to the 'Cappadocians', who were a nation in what is now southern Turkey. The 'Medes' came from an area which undoubtedly would be northern Iran and perhaps part of eastern Afghanistan and southern Turkey. Javan seems to be associated with Greece. This subject will be further examined in the chapter entitled 'The Arab League.

The obvious question about Gog comes to mind, since there are so few actual references to this name in the scripture, 'Is this Gog of Ezekiel the same Gog that we find in Revelation 20:8,9?' I don't think so for a number of reasons, which I have listed on the following pages, that reflect differences between the two references.

DIFFERENCES

Between Gog of Revelation and Gog of Ezekiel

REVELATION 20	**EZEKIEL 38,39**
SATAN draws Gog and Magog together against the camp of the Saints.	The LORD draws Gog and Magog together against Israel
Fire comes down from heaven in judgement on them.	Internal strife causes them to kill one another with the sword before the brimstone.
Their bodies are consumed by the fire from Heaven.	Their bodies become birdfood for the fowls of the air.
They are gathered on the 'broad plain of the earth'.	They are gathered on the 'mountains of Israel'.
They surround the camp of the Saints.	They surround Israel, restored from the nations.
The time is after the 1000 year Millennial period.	The time is at the close of the Tribulation Period, and before the Millennium.

I don't remember reading about anyone that intermixed these two battles of Gog, but I feel a distinction needs to be established anyway. A few questions remain: When *does* Ezekiel's battle of Gog and Magog take place (time wise), and are we supposed to watch for it? Does Russia really go into the Middle East after oil? How does this battle of Gog fit with the book of Revelation, aside from chapter 20? The following comparison notes the similarities between Armageddon and Ezekiel chapter 38 & 39

SIMILARITIES
Of Gog's Battle (Ezek.) and Armageddon (Rev.)

GOG'S BATTLE(Ezekiel)	ARMAGEDDON (Rev.)
The Lord brings Gog and Magog with hooks in the jaw into the battle(Ez.38:4).	The Lord brings Antichrist into battle with evil spirits from his mouth.(Rv.16:4).
Battle is fought on the mountainsof Israel(Ez.38:8). and (Ez.39:4).	Battle is fought at Armageddon(Rv.16:16).outsidethe city (Rv.14:19,20)
Thoughts are put into his mind to devise an evil plan (Ez.38:10)	God puts it into their hearts to execute His purpose.(Rv.17:17).
The Lord's fury mounts up in His anger(Ez.38:18).	The wrath of God is mixed to full strength in cup of His anger. (Rv.14:10).
A great earthquake in the land of Israel(Ez.38:19).	A great earthquake such as man has never seen before (Rv.16:18).
Man and beast, fowl and fish quake at His presence (Ez.38:20).	Kings and great men hide themselves from His presence (Rv.6:15,16).
Hailstones.(Ez.38:22).	Hailstones.(Rv.16:21)
A mighty army riding on horses.(Ez.38:15)	An army of 200 million horsemen. (Rv.9:17).
Much blood is spilled (Ez. 38:22).	Blood flows for 200 miles (Rv.14:20).

'My Table' is the flesh of the fallen army(Ez.39:20).	'The great supper of God' is the flesh of the army (Rv.19:17,18).
Every kind of bird is gathered by Lord to eat flesh and drink blood(Ez.39:17).	All the birds of the air are assembled for the feast of flesh.(Rv.19:17,18).
Fire upon Magog and the coastlands. (Ez.39:6).	The Lord smites the nations.(Rv.19:15)
All nations will see My Glory (Ez.39:21).	Host of heaven say Hallelujah. 24 elders say Hallelujah. A great multitude says Hallelujah (Rv.19:1-6).
The Lord physically appears and becomes Israel's God. (Ez.37:26,27,28).	The Lord physically appears on Mt.Zion (Rv.14:1) then on a white horse(Rv.19:11).

One of the most dramatic of all prophecies in the Bible occurs in these portions, where God calls all nations together against Israel in one last great battle. The wrath of the LORD reaches its fullness, and He **personally** comes to the aid of Israel, in a Theophanes unparalleled in the history of time itself, bringing forth judgement with the sword, pestilence, fire and brimstone, and spilled blood flows like a river. Israel will finally receive Messiah as a nation, and He will receive them. The words of EZEK.37:27 ring forth with a glorious paean of triumph '**I will be their God, and they will be My people**'. Both of these two scriptures are revealing the exact same event, which will occur at the end of the Tribulation, and will be known as the 'Battle of Armageddon'.

5.

OLIVET REVISITED

This chapter contains a rather brief analysis of the prophetic teaching that the Lord Jesus delivered to the disciples while on the Mount of Olives, and which was recorded for us in Matthew 24, Mark 13, and Luke 21.

Ironic as it may be, the doctrine of the 2nd advent, as taught by the Lord in Mt.24, is probably the most misinterpreted and misunderstood prophetic passage in the entire Bible, even though it is probably the most familiar. It would seem logical to suppose that Jesus teaching on His own return would be the clearest teaching on the subject, but this may not be the case. The method of interpretation of this passage known as 'The Olivet Discourse' , will ultimately determine its understanding. By that I mean, that if you begin the study of this chapter with a theological viewpoint of a 'pre-trib dispensationalist', you will conclude that the chapter is speaking of that very thing. If, on the other hand, if you hold to a WYSIWYG (What You See Is What You Get) view, then your conclusions will favor a post-tribulation viewpoint.

I have been taught that Matthew 24 did not pertain to the church at all, but rather to a remnant of Jews that believed in Christ after the translation of 'true believers' had taken place in what is often called 'The Rapture'. The prophecies of 'doom and gloom' really applied to 'someone else', since a 'true believer' was not to be around to witness those dreadful things. Israel was the fig tree, and since this generation has seen

Israel become a nation and grow as prophesied in scripture, then I as a 'true believer' would be among the generation (about 30 years) that would quite probably be alive when the Lord returned. Lets see now, 1947 plus 30 = 1977. OK!, so maybe a generation is a little longer than 30 years.

This chapter is a brief analysis of the context of Mat.24, which we must include in any prophetic study of the second coming of our Lord. Since Jesus is explaining to his closest four disciples, what the sequence of events leading up to His return are going to be, it seems logical, that He would have the best explanation in all of Biblical prophecy. The two sets of brothers, James and John, Peter and Andrew, along with Jesus, were coming out of the temple, when they pointed out the marvelous stones, and wonderful buildings, and how it was adorned with votive gifts. Indeed, some of the stones of Herod's temple still exist today, and reveal the care of stone cutters, who even carved borders on each stone. Jesus used the opportunity to teach prophetically, what would happen to the temple stones, as He said, '...not one stone here shall be left upon another, which will not be torn down.' (Mt.24:2). They crossed the Kidron valley, and came to the Mount of Olives, where Jesus often went, and as they were sitting there, the disciples inquired further into the statement that Jesus had made earlier.

Mat.24:3

> *And as He was sitting on the Mount of Olives, the disciples came to Him privately, saying, 'Tell us, when will these things be, and what will be the sign of Your coming and the end of the age?'*

I suppose if I had been one of the disciples, I might have asked the same question. Consider, that the temple was the very embodiment of what Judaism was all about, and that Herod had spent 40 years remodeling it with ornate and costly workmanship along with much gold. It was a marvelous work, but then Jesus informs them that not one stone would be left standing. In addition, we find that Jesus had taught them on earlier occasions about the kingdom of heaven, as a day of judgement, hell, persecution, a gathering of tares by reaping angels, His own death at Jerusalem, His coming in glory, the coming of Elijah, His resurrection on the third day, and judgement upon this generation. When is all the going to happen? What are you talking about? Is this magnificent temple actually going to be torn down? When are you coming to claim your rightful throne as king of Israel? What are the signs that will give us a clue that the kingdom is coming? I think the disciples were quite surprised to learn about the temple being destroyed, and they wanted to know more about it.

The prophecy concerning the temple stones was remarkably fulfilled about 35 years later (70 AD), when Titus destroyed the city of Jerusalem, and because of this historical event, many people have interpreted Mat.24 as past history. The obvious difficulty in that postulation, is that not all of it has yet happened, since it ultimately ends with a Theophanes (that is the appearance of God), Mt.24:30.

Jesus said,'...see to it that no one misleads you.' (Mt.24:4). Who was He talking to? Unsaved Jews that would be on the scene some 2000 years later? I think He was talking to His disciples. He didn't want them to be misled, and I think that thought still caries through to His disciples today.

We are often taught this famous parable; '...as it was in the days of Noah' Mt.24:37, by nearly every commentator who has written about the second coming of Christ, where an unexpected arrival catches some off guard, and catches true believers away. Books have been written describing airplanes whose born again pilots suddenly disappear, leaving the plane full of sinners to get themselves down. Automobiles without drivers, plunging into busy intersections because the Christian driver has been 'raptured' just before the light changed. If you have read books about the end times, you may be familiar with the scenario described, which certainly makes sensational, spectacular, and interesting reading.

In the passage we cited, the thought continues;

Mt.24:40,41

Then there shall be two men in the field; one will be taken, and one will be left. Two women will be grinding at the mill; one will be taken and one will be left.

This passage is used by many to illustrate that the rapture will take one and leave the other to go through the great tribulation. Lets look at the preceding verses for a moment.

Mt.24:37.38.39

For the coming of the Son of Man will be just like the days of Noah. For as in those days which were before the flood they were eating and drinking, they were marrying and giving in marriage, until the day of Noah entered the ark. and they did not understand until the flood came and took them all away, so shall the coming of the Son of Man be.

Now, who are the ones taken away and who were the ones left? Our natural 'pretrib' instinct is to say that Noah was taken - but is that what it says? No! Noah was the one that understood what was happening because God had told him in advance, exactly what He was going to do, when the rain would start, and how long it would last. (Gen.7:1-4). The ones that did not understand were the same ones that were unaware of the impending judgement and were conducting business as usual, that were taken away. That is the way the coming (parousia)[1] of the Son of Man will occur. In a word, 'unexpected'. I refer to the greek word for coming, since it is the exact word used in verse 24:27 and 24:30, in which the coming

---

[1] **παρουσια**

of the Son of Man is as a lightening flash across the entire sky, when all tribes of the earth will mourn when they see the Son of Man coming on clouds of the sky with power and glory. I have thought that since the 2nd coming was to be imminent, that I would not **know** when He was coming, hence the element of surprise would be there. While we have a definite admonishment for preparedness (Mt.24:44), the point is that the 'they' of (Mt.24:39) who did not 'understand' was not Noah, but the ones 'taken away' by the flood. The two succeeding verses carry the thought further, with the two men in the field, and the two women at the mill. I have also used these verses many times to demonstrate a pretrib rapture, without realizing my interpretation was exactly backwards, and while it as an obvious fact that the ones taken were taken in judgement, it was a major revelation to me. When we examine the whole book of Matthew concerning what Jesus had previously taught about the subject, we discover an amazing thing. The unrighteous are taken from among the righteous before the righteous are gathered. The parable of the sower (Mt 13:24-30)

Mt.13:30

> *'...first gather the tares; and bind them in bundles to burn them up; but gather the wheat into my barn.'*

Jesus explains this parable Mt.13:39-42, where the identity of the illustration is made:

the enemy = the devil
the harvest = the end of the age
the reapers = angels
the tares = sons of the evil one
the wheat = children of God.
the furnace of fire implies hell.

To conclude the illustration, a summary is made

Mt. 13:49,50

> *So it will be at the end of the age; the angels shall come forth, and take out the wicked from*

> *among the righteous, and will cast them into the furnace of fire; there shall be weeping and gnashing of teeth.*

The typical dispensational position is to place these prophecies of Christ into a Jewish context and thus eliminate the obvious problem. If the rapture came first and removed the Church before the tribulation, then the Matthew passages could be relegated to faithful Jews who would pass through the Tribulation, and be left after the removal of the ungodly at the climax of the tribulation. This all sounds good from a Church position before the tribulation, but unfortunately, it is not what the Bible teaches. While I am immensely indebted to the laborious efforts of many saintly dispensationalists, I cannot lend affirmation to conjectural theory of this magnitude with the only means of support being that it "sounds good". Furthermore, I am reminded with fear and trembling, that adopting a theological concept just because that is the way I would like it to be, is extremely dangerous.

2 Tim.4:3,4

> *For the time will come when they will not endure sound doctrine; but wanting to have their ears tickled, they will accumulate for themselves teachers in accordance to their own desires; And will turn away their ears from the truth, and will turn aside to myths.*

Luke also records the same examples used of Noah, Lot and the two women at the mill in (Luke 17:26-35), and recounts that one is taken and one is left. Since the context and illustration are the same, we presume the instrument to be the same also.

On a somewhat humorous note, Jesus, immediately after explaining to the disciples about the parables, asked them (Mt.13:51),"Have you understood all these things: they said to Him,'Yes'." Perhaps they did indeed understand, or perhaps they understood all they were taught up to that point in time. Interesting also, is the fact that every incidence where Jesus taught the disciples about prophetic events to come, always related to a post-trib, pre-mill second advent.

(Mt.24:29,30) "...after the tribulation of those days..." astronomical signs will occur that will result in the sign of the ages, the appearance of the Son of Man in the sky, coming in clouds of glory, and "... all the tribes of the earth will mourn, and they will see..."

Some will be quick to point out that Matthew uses the term 'kingdom of heaven' while Mark, Luke, and John use the term 'Kingdom of God', and that the distinction of these two kingdoms is sufficient to answer the question of 'who is taken and who is left', by relating the kingdom of heaven to a view including the quashing of the insurgency initiated by Satan after the millennium (Rev.20:8-10). This is a possible solution, yet some of the same parables,i.e. (Mt.19:14, Lk.18:16, Mt.13:33, Lk.13:21, Mt.13:31, Mk.4:30), as a few examples, are used by the Lord to teach a truth about a kingdom in another realm. It seems unlikely to me that the Lord Jesus would make one statement that could be later separated to teach two different concepts. Should we go to another kingdom, when He makes reference to "my" kingdom, (Jn.18:36)? My only point is that I think too much is made of the terminology from one gospel to another that wasn't really there when it was initially taught by the Lord. To subsequently press this into a theological explanation of an admittedly difficult text is 'begging the question;', and I think we should look elsewhere for an acceptable explanation.

Perhaps the question of who is taken and who is left is not really that difficult after all. I see the return of the Lord and our gathering to Him as a punctilious event. That is - it takes place within the frame of a relatively short period of time. Mt.13:39 (ff) may not be that way at all, but may be spread out over the whole seven year period. Indeed, the angels are sent to execute God's judgement throughout the entire seven year period of tribulation.

Mt. 13:49

So it will be at the end of the age; the angels shall come forth, and take out the wicked from among the righteous,"...

This is not really a reversed rapture, as I had first imagined, but rather a general condition that takes place during the course of the tribulation. The Church is still there, awaiting the return of the King, while the angels are busy removing the tares from the harvest. Even after the King comes, and receives unto himself the subjects of His kingdom, the angels are still busy collecting the tares. The last seven bowls of the wrath of God are poured out and God, in His mercy, and in the midst of judgement is still looking for a demonstration of acknowledgement of His Lordship, and yet most of mankind still refuses Him.

They worshipped the image of the beast(Rev.16:2). They "...did not repent, do as to give Him glory." Rev.16:9 "...they blasphemed the God of heaven because of their pain and their sores; And they did not repent of their deeds." (Rev.16:11) Even at the very last "...and men blasphemed God because of the plagues of the hail..."(Rev.16:21).

The refrain of Isaiah 9 and 10 comes to mind, as it is often repeated.

"...In spite of all this His anger does not turn away, and His hand is still stretched out."

A matter of guidance

Mt.24:4"...see to it that no one misleads you". This pertains to wandering, deception, fraud, perverseness, seduction, and sin. The admonition by the Lord is a warning to be alert in the end times, because it will be possible to be deceived and misled. (Mt.24:10,11,12,23,24,26) have inherent, if not specific caution against deception in the last days. Some impostors, even being so brazen as to come in Christ's name, saying "...I am the Christ." (Mt.24:5). It sounds absurd, yet many will be deceived, as the verse continues, "...and will mislead many."

Fig Newtons

If I asked most evangelicals this question, "Do you know about the sign of the fig tree?", the reply would most likely be something like this: "Sure!- Israel is the fig tree, and just like the fig tree blossoms, so Israel blossoms in the land in the last days." They may further add, that it is a prophecy that comes from Matthew 24, that has been fulfilled since Israel became a nation, in 1948, and it proves that Jesus is coming back in this generation. I think that a lot of Christians believe that concept, and some would even add a rather curious typeology of Israel being compared to a Jewish boy who becomes a man at 13 and goes off to war, etc.

I have heard this so many times that I have just assumed it was true based on the number of times I've heard it used. I don't have a lot of old books, but the oldest reference to this concept that I can find is in a book I respect quite highly, by Clarence Larkin, which says;

> "The fig tree is a new testament symbol or figure of Israel and was used by Jesus Himself."[1]

Matthew 24:32,33

> *Now learn the parable from the fig tree: when its branch has already become tender, and puts forth its leaves, you know that summer is near; even so you too, when you see all these things, recognize that He is near, right at the door.*

There is a problem here! For one thing,This verse doesn't say anything about Israel, and another, Jesus was talking about a parable not a sign. I know some are going to say..so what's the

---

1 Clarence Larkin, *Dispensational Truth,* 1919, page 156

difference, it all means the same. There is a very significant distinction between these two words, because the parable of the fig tree was used as an 'audio-visual' illustration of the signs that Jesus had just taught them about. I don't mean to say that the application to Israel doesn't fit, but that we have pushed a simple illustration by the Lord to mean more than what He originally intended to convey. So what was He saying by the parable? Simply that when the signs he had just told them about begin to unfold, then the time of His coming was to be considered near. Please note here, that the fig tree illustrated the proximity of specific events - of which Jewish Nationalism is not mentioned. If the church does not go through the tribulation that Jesus was talking about in Mat. 24, then you need to come up with a different explanation of the chapter, which is why the fig tree concept came into being. If Jesus intended the signs He was teaching the disciples to pertain to the Church, then - the Church WILL go through the tribulation, because the signs He gave the disciples are signs that occur during the tribulation.

If Jesus had been in Toronto, He might have used a parable of a maple tree instead of a fig tree to illustrate the point, and it might have gone something like this: When you see the seed pods falling off the maple trees, you know that it's time for the Stanley Cup Playoffs.

Some have used Jeremiah 29:17 as a proof text that Israel is the fig tree, - but even though the reference was to Israel, it was not a fig tree but like split open figs that cannot be eaten due to rottenness. The illustration is that of being unpalatable or better yet...utterly useless!

Another reference is Jeremiah 24:1-3, where Jeremiah is shown two baskets of figs. One containing good figs, and the other containing rotten figs. The good figs were a picture of the captives that would be taken to Babylon, but who would again be brought into the land. The rotten figs were like Zedekiah and Jerusalem, that were so spiritually rotten that the

Lord abandoned them.

Again, in (Rev. 6:13) the fig tree is used parabolically, but here the reference is made to the stars of the sky falling like unripe figs in a windstorm. Here we have astronomical changes taking place in the heavens with the sun, moon, and stars,...and that's all he is saying by the illustration.

I have heard radio ministers say that since we are the generation that has seen Israel go back into the land, and since Israel is the fig tree, then Jesus is coming back in this generation. This may make for exciting, sensational preaching, but it doesn't make very sound Biblical exegesis.

OK wise guy! What does the fig tree mean as it is used in Matthew 24? Well...I don't think that the Lord Jesus was intentionally trying to hide a part of theology as important as the Pre-Trib rapture with a fig tree mask. Especially when He later makes the statement, (Mark 13:23) "But take heed; behold, I have told you everything in advance."[2]
I think rather, that He is trying to illustrate the manner in which the proximity of the signs He had just taught them about, would take place. The significance of this is that the signs He was talking about occur during the tribulation period, so if they applied to the disciples, and hence to us, then it follows that the church will go through the tribulation.

I believe that the signs of Matthew 24 *are* consistent with the rest of end time prophecy, and that they do, in fact, have significance to us, and that the fig tree, is meant only as an illustration of the proximity of the signs to the 2nd advent. To add more than this, is to process the fig tree blossoms and end up with fig newtons.

---

[2] Mark 13 and Luke 21 are parallel accounts.

The great divorce

Even the word 'divorce' doesn't set very well in christian morals, as it carries with it a tenor of discontinuity of that which is eternally intended with the original marriage contract. Spiritually it suggests a discontinuity of the work of grace in an individuals life and for that reason, is not well received by my Calvinistic viewpoint. However, there will be a falling away from the faith in the 'end times'. I have often heard preachers tell about a great revival in the last days, even as the chorus goes -'there's gonna be a revival - in the land'. Make no mistake, while we desperately need and pray for revival, the last days will be characterized by a falling away from the truth.

I know that if I asked most christians to tell me about 'love', I would be referred back to ICor.13 and told about agape' love as coming only from God. If I then asked "is it possible to have agape' love without being a christian? " , most people would say no and cite a scripture reference like (Rom 5:5), "...because the love of God has been poured out within our hearts through the Holy Spirit who was given to us.", and relate that the word love here is (agape')[3] and it is only given as a result of the work of the Holy Spirit, and that can only be there when the person becomes a born again christian. This is common knowledge to even relatively new christians. The rub comes when we look at verses like (Mt.24:12), in which the word for 'love' is the very same word 'agape'.

Mt.24:12

And because lawlessness is increased, most peoples' love will grow cold.

This verse has been painful for me for several reasons:

---

[3] **(αγαπη)**

1.) If the church, along with the Holy Spirit left with a pre-trib rapture, how could those left even **have** agape' love?

2.) If the church remained into the tribulation, and the 'falling away' occurred among those that possessed (**αγαπη**) , it leaves my 'security' as a believer a whole lot more tenuous than my five point Calvinist viewpoint feels comfortable with.

3.) It doesn't lend much credence to the concept of a great revival before the rapture of the church.

The word for 'lawlessness' or 'iniquity'(KJV) is (**ανομιαν**), which literally means with out the law. This verse (Mt.24:12), is saying more than a rise in the crime rate, it is saying that there will be an increase of 'no law'. Suppose (hypothetically), that our government failed, from the top right down to the local government. Without any government, there would be no money to pay those who enforce the law, such as city police, state police, federal marshals, FBI, etc. Without the enforcement of the law, people would no longer be restrained by the threat of getting caught, and would do whatever they wanted. In 1967, when the riots engulfed our large cities, and before the National Guard was deployed, the police were told not to shoot rioters. Rioters, knowing full well that the police would not shoot them, brazenly broke into stores, stole whatever they felt like, and then burned the building. Detroit looked like a war zone, and the smoke of burning buildings could be seen for miles around. Laws are made to keep evildoers in check and to protect the innocent. Without law, sin runs its course uncontested.

scandals

Mt.24:10

And at that time, many will 'fall away' and will betray one another and hate one another

The word used for 'fall away'[4] is an interesting word, from which we get our english word 'scandal'. It is defined "cause to be caught or to fall, i.e. cause to sin (the sin may consist in a breach of the moral law, in unbelief, or in the acceptance of false teachings"[5] This is interesting in light of the moral scandals that have racked the church in 1988, much to our shame and embarrassment. I am not implying that the moral problems in our generation have any bearing on the interpretation of this verse, I am merely pointing out what it says.

Another point is the use of the word 'you'. Since the disciples had asked the question to Jesus personally, Jesus answered them personally, and spoke as if the disciples would personally be involved. Since the fall of Jerusalem partially fulfilled many of these prophecies, it seems likely many were still alive in 70 A.D. when Jerusalem fell. The Destruction of Jerusalem in 70 A.D. did not fulfill **all** these prophecies, even though more fulfillment can be seen in Luke. The point here is, that because He was addressing the disciples, it follows that 'you' referred to the disciples, at least in some associative way.

Briefly recapping the general condition of the believers in the Mt. 24, Mark 13, Luke21 'Olivet Discourse', we note:

1.) They will be delivered up to tribulation.
2.) Many believers will be killed.
3.) They will be hated by all nations.
4.) Many will fall away from the faith.
5.) Many will betray and hate one another.
6.) False prophets will mislead many.
7.) False christs will mislead many.
8.) Most believers agape' love will turn cold.
9.) Scandals will be a source of bitterness and hatred.

---

4 (σκανδαλισθησονται)

5 Arndt and Gingrich, pg.760

10.) They will be arrested and placed before courts.
11.) They will be flogged in synagogues.
12.) They will deliver up members of their own family to death.

In the midst of these things are famine, earthquakes, and wars, and on top of that, it speaks about the spreading of the 'gospel'. "..and this gospel must first be preached to all the nations"(Mark13), or if you see a difference with the kingdom message, "...and this gospel of the kingdom shall be preached in the whole world for a witness to all the nations, and then the end shall come."(Mt.24). It would appear that an incredible task will be accomplished by unsaved Jewish believers, who, without the aid of the Holy Spirit, and in the midst of this persecution, could accomplish in 3 1/2 years, that which the church without the tribulation and with the Holy Spirit has not been able to accomplish in over 1900 years. Someone is thinking.'but wait!..that is the job that the 144,000 selected Jewish evangelists will accomplish, everybody knows that!',right? This all sounds good, except for one thing: The Bible never says they are evangelists. What it does say, is that:

1.) They are marked or sealed in their forehead (Rev.7:3), with the name of the lamb, and the name of His father.(Rev.14:1).
2.) 12,000 are marked from each of the 12 tribes of Israel, (Rev.7:4-10).
3.) They sing a new song before the throne (Rev.14:3).
4.) They are celibate (unmarried) males. (Rev.14:4).
5.) They follow the Lamb where ever He goes (Rev.14:3).
6.) They don't lie, and are blameless.(Rev.14:5).

But nowhere do we read that these are the evangelists responsible for the multitudes that come to Christ during the tribulation. Ok! now what? If the church hasn't accomplished the job in almost 2000 years, and the Jews of the tribulation aren't saved, and the 144,000 are busy following the Lamb around, how do the multitudes become believers? Who tells them what to do? God is going to get the job accomplished by other beings than man.

Rev. 14:6,7

> *And I saw another angel flying in midheaven, having an eternal gospel to preach to those who live on the earth, and to every nation and tribe and tongue and people; And He said with a loud voice, "fear God, and give Him glory, because the hour of His judgement has come; and worship Him who made the heaven and the earth and the sea and the springs of waters.*

Another verse of Mt.24 that I never quite understood before, was verse 28.

The Carcass

Mt.24:28

> *Wherever the corpse is, there the vultures will gather together*
>
> KJV has "...wheresoever the carcass is, there will the eagles be gathered together."

At first this verse seems rather removed from the rest of the chapter, but after surveying all the rest of prophecy in the entire bible on the subject of the last times, it is obvious that the Lord is here referring to the great carnage at the climax of the battle of armageddon. This occasion is mentioned many times in the bible and is called by various names.. In Revelation 19 it is called 'the great supper of God', in Isaiah 34 it is called the 'sacrifice in Bozrah', in Ezekiel 39, it's called 'My sacrifice, and 'My Table'. In all these cases, the predatory birds of the air are gathered to feast on the bodies of the slain militia of the antichrist at the consummation of the Armageddon campaign.

The great omission of Jesus

It is totally untenable, that the Lord Jesus, when asked a personal question about His return by his closest followers, would intentionally mask the single, most significant event the world would ever see since its creation. It is inconceivable that Jesus would intentionally lie to His trusted friends (who would ultimately give their very lives for his cause), by failing to tell the truth about the rapture of the Church, when He had specifically said "...I have told you everything in advance"(Mk.13:23). We are clearly faced with a dilemma; either Jesus intentionally deceived the church, in which case the whole of christian doctrine falls with it like a house of cards, or - He **did** tell them everything, in which case, the Church **will** go through the tribulation, for He most certainly did not say that it would not.

The great deliverance

Lk.21:20,21

> *But when you see Jerusalem surrounded by armies, then recognize that her desolation is at hand. Then let those who are in Judea flee to the mountains, and let those who are in the midst of the city depart, and let not those who are in the country enter the city;*

In each of the parallel passages on the discourse, a similar verse is found. We have selected Luke because of a thought that I had several years ago when reading this prophetic portion of scripture. When reading through Acts, we find that Peter preached a sermon and had 3000 converts (Acts.2:41); and that daily, people were being saved and added to the church (Acts 2:47); Peter, again preaching about the resurrection, even at the expense of being jailed, had 5,000 male converts (Acts 4:4). Even in just these first few chapters of Acts, we find that the church experienced a tremendous growth which was accompanied by miracles and marvelous demonstrations of the Holy Spirit that convicted and converted over 8,000 people. Yes, there was much opposition and yes, the disciples paid dearly for their faith, but the church was experiencing an unparalleled growth explosion. These verses bring a paean of praise to my soul, and a song of rejoicing to my spirit, but then I began to trace the historic events surrounding the diaspora, and my rejoicing was saddened to grief. I learn of the destruction of Jerusalem in 70 AD by Titus and the Roman army from the historical accounts such as Flavius Josephus, and read of unimaginable horrors. My heart was heavy, my spirit grieved, and I wondered, what happened to my brothers and sisters that experienced the great growth explosion of the church less than 35 years earlier? Were they trapped in the crossfire of monstrous proportions? Did they join the ranks of the Jewish zealots that fought for the survival of the nation? Did they become innocent victims of a monumental conflagration unparalleled until recent times? What happened to those who had daily devoted themselves to the apostles teaching, fellowship, breaking of bread and prayer, and who with one mind ate together with gladness and sincerity of heart? I know they happened upon hard times, for the apostle Paul records that collections be made for the suffering saints in Jerusalem, - but they were still there. Were these suffering saints in Jerusalem wise enough to heed the warnings that Jesus prophetically made concerning the 'last days', and apply it to themselves in a prefiguration of the final days preceding the second advent? The scripture doesn't give us many clues as to their circumstances, even though the last NT book was written over 20 years after the destruction of Jerusalem took place. I did some research on early church historians, and what I found brought tears to my eyes. I am going to take the liberty of quoting some of what I found, since I know most of the readers of this book will probably not investigate this matter.

"About this time, according to the tradition recorded by the Church historian Eusebius, the Christian community within Jerusalem - the Fathers of the Church - escaped from the doomed city. They made their way across the river Jordan and took refuge in the Gentile city of Pella, 60 miles to the north-east of Jerusalem."[6] Furneaux does not respect the credence of the report by Eusebius, and suggests several reasons why this could not be, and speculates the Christians remained in the city and fought[7] "It seems probable that the christians remained in Jerusalem sharing their countrymen's glorious cause. Like their friends the Zealots, they were buoyed up by hopes of divine deliverance."[8] This conjecture is just that, and fails to realize the true nature of the Christian moral aside from the obvious error in "their friends". A further investigation into what Eusebius actually wrote reveals a little different slant on things:

"Furthermore, the members of the Jerusalem church, by means of an oracle given by revelation to acceptable persons there, were ordered to leave the city before the war began and settle in a town in Peraea called Pella. To Pella, those who believed in Christ migrated from Jerusalem; and as if holy men had utterly abandoned the royal metropolis of the Jews and the entire Jewish land, the judgement of God at last overtook them for their abominable crimes against Christ and His apostles, completely blotting out that wicked generation from among men."[9] "in computing the whole number of those who lost their lives, the historian says famine and the sword destroyed 1,100,000 persons;"[10] [that figure comes from Josephus, and may be somewhat exaggerated. hlm.]

---

[6] Furneaux, *The Roman Siege of Jerusalem*, pg.146

[7] Furneaux, op.cit.

[8] Furneaux, op.cit.

[9] Eusebius, *The History of the Church...*,pg.111

[10] Eusebius, op.cit.

Eusebius was the foremost church historian from the earliest period of the church[11] and his research is very significant to me. When I first discovered the fact, that the church was not in Jerusalem when the conflagration occurred, it brought tears to my eyes, and it reminded me that the Lord Jesus Christ is in control, and He hasn't left us in despair and without hope. We may not always be protected from the world, but we most certainly will not be judged along with it. In the quotation, Eusebius, notes that an 'oracle' was given by revelation. What he is saying here, is that God spoke to his church through prophecy, and warned them of the impending judgement that was to befall Jerusalem. The sign of the army surrounding Jerusalem came in 68 AD with Vaspasian, the Roman general who was ready to finish his Palestine campaign at that time. News from Rome forced him to return home and assume control of the country. During those two years, between 68 and 70 AD, the church having had the prophecy in their midst with the accompanying signs, left the city!

Heb.10:25

> *not forsaking our own assembling together, as is the habit of some but encouraging one another; and all the more, as you see the day drawing near.*

I never considered that this verse was more than a directive for the church to meet together until I read Eusebius' account of the 'oracle' that happened in the church at Jerusalem before 70 AD. I am convinced that God **will** speak to His people in the last days and tell them what they need to know. The key is that they are to meet together more often as they see the time of the end drawing nearer. I'm sure that the christians in the Jerusalem church were glad they met together, when they learned that God spoke in the assembly, and told them to start moving out.

---

[11] Eusebius,op.cit. introduction by Williamson.

6.

THE RAPTURE?

The portion of prophetic scripture that I have quoted and made reference to more than any other has, beyond any doubt, been I Thes. 4:14-18. It has been used by more preachers, teachers, and bible students to teach the 'rapture' than any other chapter, or verse.

I Thes.4:14-17;

> *For if we believe that Jesus died and rose again, even so God will bring with Him those who have fallen asleep in Jesus. For this we say to you by the word of the Lord, that we who are alive, and remain until the coming of the Lord, shall not precede those who have fallen asleep. For the Lord Himself will descent from heaven with a shout, with the voice of with the voice of the archangel, and with the trumpet of God; and the dead in Christ shall rise first. Then we who are alive and remain shall be caught up together with them in the clouds to meet the Lord in the air, and thus we shall always be with the Lord.*

I has been an amazement to me, that a doctrine so important to the church as the rapture, would not be specifically mentioned somewhere in scripture. I mean, the word 'rapture' itself, is not mentioned anywhere. We say, that the word comes from a French word, (actually I think it comes from a Latin word 'raptus'), but anyway, we say that this is the text that means what the word *is*, a catching away of the church both alive and dead, when Jesus comes back to earth seven years before the second advent. There will be a bodily, physical resurrection of the dead in christ at that time, and a physical transformation of the living believers, who will be given new bodies before they have left the old one by death. If this sounds like a 'science fiction' novel of a few years ago, then hang onto your hat, there are surprises ahead. The problem I have, is that I can't teach a pre-trib rapture from this passage of scripture, because it simply doesn't say that the Lord will make a secret appearance before the second advent. It may be that He will, have two stages to His second coming, but one would be hard pressed to prove it from this passage. I don't believe we should read into the scripture concepts that we think should be there. In spite of how much I may wish that this portion of scripture taught the rapture, it simply doesn't say that the second coming will be a two stage event, with a seven year gap in the middle, so we must analyze the facts that are available, and see it they make any sense without adding anything to them. You don't need to consult Ramm[1], to find out that you are on dangerous ground by adding to the Word, and a quick check of Revelation 22:18,19 or Deut.4:2 should encourage one to stick to the text. At one time I attempted to equate the greek word (parousia)[2] which is translated as 'coming' or 'presence', specifically to the rapture, but was totally unsuccessful because quite simply, it just doesn't mean that at all. My favorite lexicon[3] does a strange thing on this word, by referring to JF Walvoord in a reference

---

[1] Bernard Ramm, *Protestant Biblical Interpretation.*

[2] **παρουσιαν**

[3] Arndt and Gingrich translation of Bauer.

to a Bib.Sac.[4] article, in an attempt to delineate a second coming with a 'hidden' coming of a divinity. It should be noted also, that the references used to develop this concept come mainly from historical, pseudepigraphal, apocryphal, and even ostraka, but not from the scriptures. If you are familiar with these two references, you can appreciate the hyperbole of scholarship in this argument, but I will pursue it no further. Another meaning is also presented by A.& G.; " of Christ, and nearly always of his Messianic Advent in glory to judge the world at the end of this age:" This meaning is accompanied with a whole host of scriptural references.[5]

the with and for argument.

In my opinion, the argument which is often taken from I Thes.3:13, '...coming ... **with** all His saints', and '...coming **for** the saints I Thes.4:14-18 [implied in context], is really an argument that 'begs the question' since it cannot be unequivocally demonstrated that they are not, in fact, the same event. The very word 'parousia' actually mitigates against the 'hidden' rapture, since it is used elsewhere to mean the coming at the end of the tribulation.[see Mt.24:27,37,39; ICor15:23; 2Thes2:8,9; James 5:7,8; 2Pet.1:16,3:4,12; 1Jn2:28].

the remainder of the equation

I think I have passed over the two words 'and remain' many times, and haven't realized what the words really were referring to. Why didn't Paul just say, 'we who are alive when the Lord returns', instead of saying '...we who are alive, <u>and remain</u>' The use of the Greek article seems to be somewhat significant in this particular instance. "The repetition of the Greek article with some word or phrase which modifies the

---

4 *Biblio Theca Sacre,* a publication of Dallas Theol. Sem.

5 Arndt and Gingrich, pg.635.**παρουσια**

noun is a device employed for emphasis..."[6] Another translation, the N.I.V. adds the word 'still'[7] to alive, which adds to the emphasis of the phrase. The word 'remaining' also carries with it the concept of 'surviving'[8] which seems to make a difference in the understanding of the whole verse. Paul is not merely contrasting being dead or alive at the coming of the Lord, he is also comparing survival and death, which takes on a whole new meaning to the verse. If that is, in fact the case, then it dovetails with the Olivet Discourse where Jesus said ,Mt.24:13 "But the one who endures to the end, it is he who shall be saved.", and identical to 'those who escape' on Mt Zion on the day of the Lord (Obadiah 17), and the same as the 'survivors' who will be left in Jerusalem after the 'My wrath' comes upon it with four severe judgments (sword, famine, wild beasts, and plague) (Ezek.14:21,22); It is every one that is 'left within the land' after the Lord's judgement in 'that day' (Isa.7-:22), and is the same event that is spoken of in Isa.4.

Isa.4:3

> *And it will come about that he who is left in Zion and remains in Jerusalem will be called holy-everyone who is recorded for life in Jerusalem.*

The KJV was an accurate translation of the Textus Receptus in 1611, but, as time went on, the meanings of words often changed, such as the word 'prevent' in this same verse. I assume that anyone who still use the KJV, are using a study bible that has 'precede' noted in the margin, for that is a much better translation in today's vernacular.

---

6 Dana and Mantey, P.148.

7 New International Version of the New Testament

8 Bagster's lexicon, (**περιλειπομενοι**)

himself

There is a poignantly salient aspect of the ministry of Jesus that was totally singular in scope. Some aspects of His ministry were shared with His disciples, and others were delegated to those who were to be spiritually conceived subsequent to His earthly ministry. There are other aspects that were His and His alone to perform.

He alone died on the cross for our sins Jn.3:16.,Acts4:12
He alone was born unique, one of a kind.[9] n.1:14
He alone prayed in the garden, Jn.17.
He alone is our high priest. Heb.6:20
He alone is our coming king. Rev.15:3
He alone comes alone with judgement and vengeance. Isa.63:3
He alone is the light of the world that illumines the hearts and minds of depraved mankind to the understanding of the Almighty Jn.7:12, Jn.12:46
He alone can 'free' mankind of the shackles of darkness and the depravity of the mind. Jn.8:36
He alone has gone to prepare a place for us. Jn.14:3

"Himself", indicates to me that He will not be sending a representative or angel, neither will His coming be a spiritual presence, but a physical, and bodily appearance. John makes the physical appearance of Jesus emphatic by saying;

2Jn:7

For many deceivers have gone out into the world, those who do not acknowledge Jesus Christ as coming in the flesh. This is the deceiver and the antichrist.

---

[9] *μονογενουσ* Jn.1:14

The shout

It seems that every time I hear someone teaching on this verse, they always refer to the 'shout' as 'come up here', as if this was identical to (Rev.4:1), in which the Apostle John is paged with a 'voice' like a trumpet that says 'come up here'. These two events are **not** the same, and in fact there are so many differences we are not going to enumerate them. Similarly the two prophets who are called to heaven with 'come up here'(Rev.11:12) do not typify the 'shout' either.

The word for 'shout'[10] means 'a cry of command'[11] and might be loosely translated **'charge!'**. It is identical with the 'call' for a sword by the Lord God against Gog on the mountains of Israel (Ezek.38:21); It is the 'battle cry' on the day of the Lord's wrath (Zeph.1:14); It is the 'war cry' and 'shout' when the Lord 'will go forth like a warrior' and 'prevail' against his enemies (Isa.42:13); And it is the Lord roaring from Zion and uttering His voice from Jerusalem (Joel 3:16).

The Voice of the Archangel

I must have read (1 Thes. 4:16,17) a hundred times, and never once realized that the 'voice of the archangel' was an entirely separate and distinct part of the 'translation' of the church. I had always thought that the shout, the voice of the archangel, and the trumpet of God all happened simultaneously in the twinkling of an eye. When the event occurs, it undoubtedly will occur quickly, but the 3 events of the passage mentioned do not occur simultaneously, and there is a time period between them. I think I just heard someone say 'uhh ohh, there he goes again! Actually, I just discovered (my opinion), that the 'voice of the archangel', is the very same as

---

[10] κελευσματι

[11] Arndt and Gingrich, pg.428

the 'strong angel' of Revelation Ch.10, that cries out with a loud voice as a 'lion roars', and 7 peals of thunder sound. He is the 7th of the angels with the trumpets, and the last one to sound the trumpet. This whole chapter is about that voice and sound, and if you read Rev.10:7 it makes perfect sense.

"but in the days of the voice of the seventh angel, when he is about to sound, then the mystery of God is finished, as He preached to His servants the prophets."

The Trumpet of God

Judging from the title of the book, you may well suspect that I would be spending some time on the topic of trumpets, and you would suspect correctly. One of the reasons this study came about in the first place was the investigation of trumpets in the scriptures. I have investigated all the scriptures that I could find that have anything to do with trumpets, and have listed those that I feel relate to the subject at hand.

1Cor 15:51,52

> *Behold, I tell you a mystery; we shall not all sleep, but we shall all be changed, in a moment, in the twinkling of an eye, at the last trumpet; for the trumpet will sound, and the dead will be raised imperishable, and we shall be changed.*

Now we all know that what Paul is telling us, is about the rapture, and that is a foregone conclusion amongst the evangelical crowd. Sleep is a euphemism for death, which will not be experienced by a group of the Lord's people when He returns, but rather, they will undergo a physical transformation without experiencing physical death. Death is a separation of the physical from the spiritual, and resurrection is a rejoining of the spiritual with a physical body. The group Paul is speaking about receive a transformed physical body in a split second, when the trumpet sounds. No problem so far, right? Ok, but what about the word 'last'. I have heard this passage explained in various ways, but the most common is to assert that it is the last of a series, such as the bell that ends a class period before the bell that starts the next. This concept always bothered me, because to me 'last' means the very last. The problem comes in accepting this word 'last' as meaning the very last, because of the 'last' trumpet of revelation occurs at the end of the tribulation, and since we don't like the thought of going through the tribulation, there must be another meaning. We know that Jesus taught about a trumpet in connection with His return with power and great glory, from the Olivet Discourse.

Mat.24:30,31

> *and then the sign of the Son of Man will appear in the sky, and then all the tribes of the earth will mourn, and they will see the SON OF MAN coming on the clouds of the sky with power and great glory.*
>
> *And He will send forth His angels with a great trumpet and they will gather together His elect form the four winds, from one end of the sky to the other.*

It doesn't take much imagination, to see the similarity between these verses, and the ones we have already mentioned. Jesus is coming with clouds in the sky, and clouds are mentioned in 1Thes.4., and in other places such as Acts, Jesus was lifted up in the clouds;

Acts 1:9

> *And after He had said these things, He was lifted up while they were looking on, and a cloud received Him out of their sight.*

While we may have many different theological concepts regarding the second coming of Christ, the book of Acts is pretty specific about the manner in which He will return, as the angels instructed the disciples in the matter;

Acts 1:10,11

The Rapture?

> *And as they were gazing intently into the sky while He was departing, behold, two men in white clothing stood beside them; and they also said, "Men of Galilee, why do you stand looking into the sky? This Jesus who has been taken up from you into heaven, will come in just the same way as you have watched Him go into heaven."*

When Jesus went to heaven, it was clearly observed by the disciples, who watched Him ascend into a cloud, and His return will be in the same manner - physical and visible.

Events of the Seventh Trumpet

It is significant to note that in the days of the seventh trumpet of Revelation 10,11, several things happen which are of direct interest and consequence to the church.

1.) The mystery of God is finished. (Rev.10:7) (see Rom.-11:25)

2.) There is a transferring of the kingdom of the world to the kingdom of the Lord. (Rev.11:15)

3.) Jesus begins to reign. (Rev.11:17)

4.) The wrath of God comes at this time. (Rev.11:18)

5.) Judgement of believing dead occurs. (Rev.11:18)

6.) Destruction of living unbelieving destroyers of the earth. (Rev.11:18)

7.) The heavenly temple of God is opened.

8.) The ark of the Covenant appears in the heavenly temple (Rev.11:19).

9.) Nature responds with lightning, earthquakes, thunder, and a great hailstorm. (Rev.11:19).

10.)A war takes place in heaven between Michael and his angels, and Lucifer and his angels. (Rev.12:7-9).

11.)The third woe occurs, which is the Devil and his angels who come down to earth with great wrath, after loosing the heavenly battle. (Rev.12:9-12).

12.)Israel,(the woman) flees to a place in the wilderness for 3 1/2 years. (Rev.12:14).

13.)The Lamb stands on Mount Zion.(Rev.14:1).

14.)The Lord is seen on a white cloud and begins His judgement on the earth. (Rev.14:14).

15.)The 7 bowls of the wrath of God are poured out. (Rev.16:1).

Chapters 12,13, and 14 of Revelation are what we might refer to as 'parenthetical', in that they may not be chronologically arranged with the preceding chapters. We read one line after another, one page after another, one chapter after another, that is, our means of understanding is 'serial'. In reality, the chronology of Revelation is not 'serial' at all, but 'parallel', or, in other words, many things are happening at the same time in different realms. This is difficult for us to comprehend, because it is like a 4th dimensional chess game, and we can only see one level. Because of this difficulty in understanding, many students of Revelation have spiritualized much of the text, or rendered it so figurative as to be mythological. Because we may not be able to stack everything in neat little piles, does not mean that we should relegate that which doesn't fit into ubiquitous metaphors.

The O.T. also has numerous references to the trumpet in connection with cataclysmic judgments during the last days.

Isa.27:13

It will come about also in that day that a great trumpet will be blown; and those who were perishing in the land of Assyria and who were scattered in the land of Egypt will come and worship the

LORD in the holy mountain at Jerusalem.

According to my 'paper tiger' theory, the argument against this verse is that it is a call to worship during the millennium, and not part of the tribulation prophecies at all. The preceding verse of (Isa.27:12), in reference to 'that day' talks about the Lord starting his threshing from the stream of the Euphrates to the brook of Egypt, and the sons of Israel being gathered one by one at that time. The word 'brook' would be somewhat a demeaning word to describe the world's longest river, if the Nile is the reference being made. It is most probable that the Nile is not the 'brook' being referred to, but rather the 'Wadi el Arish',[12] which is in the Sinai to the West of Israel's (current) south-western border, and which empties into the Mediterranean Sea. I find it totally fascinating that even the locations of the last great battles are given in scripture.

Zeph.1:16

A day of trumpet and battle cry, Against fortified cities, and the high corner towers.

We have already made mention of this verse in connection with the battle cry, but it is strikingly significant that the trumpet is also mentioned here, in connection with the 'day of the Lord'. It is listed here, as a day of 'wrath', 'trouble', 'distress', 'darkness', 'gloom', 'clouds', 'thick darkness', 'trumpet', and 'battle cry'. There will be great distress, and blood will be poured out like 'dust', and nothing will be able to deliver them from the wrath of the Lord. He will come with a vengeance, with jealousy, and He will make a complete end of 'all' the inhabitants of the earth. The mercy of the Lord is a constant amazement to me, and I marvel at His grace and wisdom, for immediately after stating that 'all the inhabitants of the earth' would be terminated, Zephaniah 2 begins by an

---

[12] Finnigan, *Light From the Ancient Past,* footnote p.130

exhortation to 'gather yourselves together' before the day of the Lord comes upon you, and 'seek the Lord', and '...Perhaps you will be hidden in the day of the Lord's anger' (Zeph.2:3). The curtain is going up on the third and final act on the stage of bible prophecy, releasing judgement to the earth through the wrath of God. If you are not sure which side of the fence you are on, I urge you to apply the blood of the passover lamb (The Lord Jesus) over the doorpost of your own life, that perhaps you may be passed over when the death angel of judgement ushers in the wrath of God.

Jer.4:19,20

> *"... Because you have heard, O my soul, the sound of the trumpet, the alarm of war. Disaster on disaster is proclaimed, for the whole land is devastated..."*

The Lord says, that 'my people' are foolish, stupid children that have no understanding, that do evil deeds and do not know how to do good, and they 'know me not'. To take this verse by itself may seem benign enough, but in the context of the entire chapter, it can only mean ***the last trump***.

Jer.49:2

> *Therefore behold, the days are coming, declares the LORD, that I shall cause a trumpet blast of war to be heard against Rabbah of the sons of Ammon; and it will become a desolate heap, and her towns will be set on fire. Then Israel will take possession of his possessors, says the LORD.*

This chapter is dedicated to describe the outcome of several arab nations, of which Ammon is the first to be mentioned. Ammon is, at the time of this writing, the nation of Jordan, which lies directly to the east of the river Jordan, between the Dead Sea, and the Sea of Galilee. The word 'Ammon' comes from the son of Lot by his youngest daughter. 'Moab', that frequently is named in connection with Ammon, was the son of

Lot by his oldest daughter, and possessed the land immediately above Ammon, and across the Jordan from Israel's northern end, and is probably considered part of Syria today. Some archaeologists claim that Ammon has been destroyed, fulfilling the prophecies; "The doom of desolation prophesied against Ammon (Ezek.25:5,10; Zeph.2:9) has been literally fulfilled. 'Nothing but ruins are found here by the amazed explorer. Not an inhabited village remains, and not an Ammonite exists on the face of the earth'"[13] However, a close examination of Zech.2, will reveal that he is speaking of 'the day of the Lord's anger', and that the 'remnant' of 'My people' will plunder them and inherit them. Israel most certainly does not possess the land of Ammon today, neither has a 'remnant' plundered the Ammonites. Further investigation in Unger's dictionary reveals that the nation of Ammon was swallowed up by Rome, but the people were still 'quite numerous' in the time of Justin Martyr (about 150 AD) and apparently merged with the Arabs about the time of Origin (186-254 AD).[14] The prophecy is yet to be fulfilled, but will become a reality when the Lord makes His dramatic entrance on the eve of the history of this dispensation, and ushers in the dawn of a new day.

Zech.9:14

> *Then the LORD will appear over them, and His arrow will go forth like lightening; and the Lord God will blow the trumpet, and will march in the storm winds of the south.*

Now who is the Lord going to appear over? and who is going to be the suffering the brunt of the Lord's storm? '...And I will stir up your sons, O Zion, against your sons, O Greece...'-

---

[13] *Unger's Bible Dictionary*, pg.45, quotes the archaeologist Thompson, *Land and Book*,iii, p.622

[14] Unger's Bible Dictionary, pg.45.

(Zech.9:13). Aha!, that's it. The antichrist comes from Greece, this verse proves it, right? Ah, well - close but no cigar. No!, the antichrist doesn't come from Greece, at least not the European Greece as we know it today. Probably one of the biggest problems I have studying biblical prophecy is staying on the topic I want to investigate. Prophecy has a way of sliding from one subject to another right in the middle of the stream, and such is this verse - which we will deal with later.

I have listed verses in the N.T. and listed verses in the O.T. that deal with the subject of the trumpet as it is blown by the Lord immediately at the commencement of His 'mop-up' campaign in the Middle East. All of these verses, in my opinion, are dealing with the exact same event, the same time, the same geographical area, and are an 'identity'. Some very eminent scholars have occluded the issue with a 'smoke screen' of scholarship and esoteric verbiage, in a futile attempt to insert a pre-trib rapture in the trumpet. Which came first, the chicken or the egg? [that's a dry joke folks]. You didn't get it? Ok, let me rephrase it. Do you take your theology, and read it into every verse in the Bible, regardless of what the text says, or do you take the verses as they come and hang the theology? It's not a simple task either way, but I rather think that many have made an argument by a technique which we may call 'special pleading', for you logic buffs, by intentionally neglecting the argument of the obvious signs.[15] [16] I highly disdain the use of any 'ad hominem' argument, and would not for an instant show disrespect for these most redoubtable of prophetic scholars. It is amazing to find other books, (than those mentioned) of voluminous content concerning the second coming, and not find much of anything concerning the issue of the trumpets. Some have speculated so wildly

---

[15] Dwight Pentecost, *Prophecy For Today*, pg.27.

[16] John F. Walvoord, *The Rapture Question*, pg.182

concerning highly subjective and speculative concepts, that (at least to me) their credibility is tarnished. Without any doubt, the most respected and profound of any that I have read, has attempted to distinguish between the trumpet of God as opposed to an angel blowing the trumpet.[17] To assert that there is a difference between an angel blowing a trumpet and the Lord blowing the trumpet is a little like this example: When our president delivers a statement to the press, he may do it through a press secretary, and while the delivery may be the act of the secretary, the president is non the less the one that is associated with the statement. An angel is, in fact a 'messenger' who is sent on specific tasks in behalf of the Lord.[18]

Conclusions of Trumpets

It is my contention that the 'great trumpet'(Mt.24), the 'trumpet of God'(1Thes.4), the 'seventh trumpet'(Rev.11), and the 'last trumpet'(1Cor.15) are, in fact, the very same and very last trumpet. In addition, I am convinced that the 'great trumpet' (Isa.27), the 'trumpet'(Zeph.1),(Zech.9),(Jer.4 & 49) are also the same very last trumpet, which is blown as a 'charge' command in which the Lord Himself, will bodily and physically enter the scene on the eve of the conclusion of the history of this age, will bring about retribution to the oppressors of Israel, draw His people around Him, and usher in the dawn of a new age.

TheAnswer

'The Answer' is really Paul's answer to the problem that the Thessalonian church was having concerning the rapture. Paul had previously visited the city, and explained to them about the second coming of Christ, and a short time later, that

---

[17] Gundry, *The Church and the Tribulation*, pg.149

[18] Bagster's Lexicon, (αγγελοσ).

church suffered persecution, and thought that they were in the great tribulation. Paul wrote 2Thes. to clarify to the church of Thessalonica his teaching concerning the second coming; to correct them in an area of doctrine that was incorrect; and also to tell them about some of the things that they were doing right. Paul compliments them for their perseverance and faith in the midst of persecution, and the fact that their love for one another was growing. We have a natural tendency to associate persecution with a declination of faith and activity, but it need not be that way, and the Thessalonians demonstrated that very fact. It is my gut feeling, that should the church go through the tribulation, as I believe it surely shall, it could be a time of increased faith and love, and a time when true believers could exercise body life without the problems and hangups of the conventional system we are part of today. Persecution has a way of causing evaluations to be made of that which is significant, and that which is superficial to the body itself. Rightly understanding the true nature and function of what the body really is, could mean the difference between survival or extinction.

Paul tells these persecuted believers that the Lord will return and execute justice to those who have afflicted them (2Thes.1-:7), when He would be 'revealed'[19] from heaven with His mighty angels, in flaming fire, and be glorified in His saints on 'that day'..

All shook up

2Thes.2:1,2

> *Now we request you, brethren, with regard to the coming of our Lord Jesus Christ, and our gathering together to Him that you may not be quickly shaken from your composure or be disturbed either by a spirit or a message or letter as if from us, to the effect that the day of the Lord has come.*

---

[19] **αποκαλυψει**

The word for coming here, is the word 'parousia'[20] that we have discussed elsewhere, and which is tied together with 'our gathering together to Him', and is used in the same context as 'the day of the Lord'. Apparently, there was a flagrant, and deceptive attempt to deceive the church of Thessalonica by attempting to convince them that the day of the Lord had already come. Paul tells them not to be shaken up, because he was not the author of the message or letter that was signed in his name, and also not to be disturbed by a spirit.

The great omission of Paul

2Thes.2:3

> *Let no one in any way deceive you, for it will not come unless the apostasy comes first, and the man of lawlessness is revealed, the son of destruction,*

Paul! What are you talking about? Lets get this straight here. The church of Thessalonica thought they were already into the tribulation, and were anticipating the parousia and gathering together (rapture) of the saints, and Paul says that it will **not** happen unless (2) things happen first! the Apostasy, and the revealing of the antichrist. Quite frankly, this section of scripture has caused me considerable difficulty, because I have tried quite unsuccessfully, to fit this into a pre-trib viewpoint. Taken literally, and at face value, this section teaches us that 2 things are going to happen **before** the rapture takes place, and that is not the doctrine of an imminent return. Others have said that the word 'apostasy'[21] really

---

20 **παρουσιαν**

21 **αποστασια**

means 'departure'[22] but most lexicons do not support this unusual definition, but rather describe apostasia as 'rebellion and abandonment'[23] and the cognate form also carries with it the idea of giving one a 'certificate of divorce'. Furthermore, Paul later writes to Timothy and uses the very same word in a context of turning from the faith unto demonology, deception, and carnal asceticism.

1Tim.4:1

> *But the Spirit explicitly says that in later times some will fall away from the faith, paying attention to deceitful spirits and doctrines of demons,...*

Additionally, Paul says that difficult times will come in the last day, and people will be characterized by attributes that are exactly opposite what you would find in (1Cor.13),(2Tim.3:1-7). Evil men will progress from a bad condition to a worse one, with much deception(2tim.3:13), and people will prefer to listen to someone teach in such a manner that they are pleased with what they hear (2Tim.4:3,4). We already know that Jesus taught about a falling away, and tough times for believers in the last days (Mt.24:10,11,12). Peter also, speaks of false teachers, and false prophets who will introduce false doctrines that many will follow (2Pet.2:1-3); and that there would be mockers who would chide people who believe that Jesus would come and bring judgement with Him (2Pet.3:3,4). John taught that antichrist, and the spirit of antichrist would come and bring doctrinal heresy,(1Jn.2:18,22; 1Jn.4:3), and that the spirit of antichrist is a deceiver, who deceives by denying that Jesus is coming in the flesh.(2Jn.7). Jude also gives an exhortation and a warning about the mockers who will appear in the last times who would give themselves to a doctrine of hedonism

---

[22] E. Schuyler English has suggested this interpretation.

[23] Arndt and Gingrich. pg.97.

(Jude 18), and encourages believers to keep the faith and pray (Jude 20).

I know this kind of material is not really very encouraging, and I don't mean to dwell on the negative. I am merely illustrating a point, that the scriptures reveal rather unanimously, that the last days are going to be pretty rough going, and we as christians should not anticipate an early removal. Who, after all, are the ones who are going to fall away? Here comes the tiger again!!! No one can fall away from something he never had in the first place - no!, it's not the unbeliever that falls away, it's believers that are totally dejected because they are going to be put 'through the fire', so to speak, of the tribulation, when they were anticipating an early dinner bell. I have always wondered about this next verse:

Eph.5:27

> *...that He might present to Himself the church in all her glory, having no spot or wrinkle or any such thing; but that she should be holy and blameless.*

The church today doesn't impress me this way at all. Sadly enough, we have had more scandals and problems than I would have even guessed possible. The church seems to be blameable for improprieties by even the unbelieving world, seems full of doctrinal wrinkles, and the bridal gown seems to have dirty smudges all over it.

Paul has missed the mark in this chapter, if the pretrib theology is correct, because he fails to directly address the rapture question with a clearly defined answer, but instead gives them 'comfort' by telling them about two signs that will come before the Lord returns, and these two signs take place about the middle of the tribulation. Some 'comfort'!! If Paul knew about a pretrib rapture of the church, and intentionally failed to communicate that truth, then his credibility is indeed tarnished. If the pretrib theory is correct and Paul didn't know about it, it places christians like J.N. Darby[24] in a position of revelation exceeding the apostle himself, which seems totally incongruous. If on the other hand, Paul did not conceal any hidden meaning in the text, and he was totally informed as to the chronology of eschatological events, then it follows that the 'straight forward' WYSIWYG (what you see is what you get) explanation of this chapter is correct, and the conclusion of that logic is a post trib rapture! Is it not more than curious, that the three people in the NT that knew more about eschatology than anyone, namely Jesus, Paul, and John, would all miss the greatest theme of the church, that is the pretrib rapture?

The restrainer

2Thes.2:6,7

> *And you know what restrains him now, so that in his time he may be revealed. For the mystery of lawlessness is already at work; only he who now restrains will do so until he is taken out of the way.*

Many different explanations have been written about the identity of the restrainer from the papacy, human government, the Holy Spirit, the church, christians, ... the list goes on. I'm not sure either, but it does seem that the first restrainer has a neuter gender 'what', and that would indicate the possibility it being God Himself. To suggest that the Holy Spirit is taken out of the way, and permits the antichrist to surface is unsupported by the rest of prophetic scripture. The phrase 'taken out of the way' is a strange translation, for a text that literally says 'out of the midst (middle) he comes'. If the 'he' refers to the Holy Spirit, then the two witnesses don't have the Holy Spirit, for they prophecy during the last 3 1/2 years, if I understand the chronology correctly (Rev.11:3). It seems

---

24 MacPherson, *The Incredible Cover-up*, pg.82 ff.

most likely that the one revealed is the antichrist, based on the context of the chapter, for Paul speaks of him being revealed (2:3,8). If the church is 'holding back the antichrist', it most certainly is without either its knowledge or conscious effort. There is only one that could be described in either neuter or masculine gender, and that is God Himself, which is my guess for the restrainer. 2Peter 3:7 also adds weight to that argument by stating "But the present heavens and earth by His word are being reserved for fire, kept for the day of judgement and destruction of ungodly men."

7.

ABOMINATION of DESOLATION

The 'Abomination of desolation' is an act by which the Antichrist and his forces, in an abhorrent manner, sacrilegiously desecrate the temple of God, (most likely in Jerusalem), at or near the end of the seven year tribulation period, and 3 & 1/2 years after the temple grain offering has been stopped..

Historically both Antiochus IV (Epiphanies) and Titus have partially typified this heinous abomination, and are livid examples of the odious nature of the act. This desecration is so blatant that it is specifically noted in Matthew 24:15, and 2 Thessalonians 2:3 as a sign which will precede the second coming of the Lord. It is not to be considered as a metaphorical illustration or obtuse spiritual degeneration, but rather a specific act at a specific time by a specific individual that will be readily identifiable by the believing community. We have already examined the scriptures concerning the source of the Antichrist's authority and power in chapter 2 (A Serpentine Trail), and observed many aspects that are unique about the character, nature and idiosyncracies of the person of antichrist in chapter 3 (Man of Sin), but it seems appropriate to examine this particular sign of abomination separately.

The LORD Himself made reference to this event, as He described the sequence of the end time events to His disciples. The 'Abomination' would be an unmistakable 'sign' to believers that they would not miss.

MATTHEW 24:15

Therefore when you see the ABOMINATION OF DESOLATION which was spoken of through Daniel the prophet, standing in THE HOLY PLACE (let the reader understand),

It is inconceivable that the LORD would say '..when you see..', and not be directly referring to the people He was addressing, or indirectly referring to future believers.

The abomination was specifically mentioned as 'standing' in the holy place', which would undoubtedly refer to the area of the temple (which is yet to be constructed), in which only the priests were allowed to enter. There is a parody here, in that only the priests were to be allowed in the holy place, yet Jesus is telling them that when 'you' see the abomination... Strictly speaking, the sign would have been observable only by those who would be allowed in the Holy Place, that is, the temple priests. This is somewhat of a paradox, since Jesus was predicting that His followers would be able to **see** the 'abomination' standing in the Holy Place, and only priests were allowed in that place. This strange scenario is so obtuse it hardly bears mentioning, yet I suppose there is a remote possibility of it occurring. The most likely explanation, is that this action of antichrist will be so well known and documented, that everyone will be aware of what has happened.

As events progress toward the culmination of the end time, the pulse of spiritual Jewish Nationalism will be monitored by the finger of spiritual members of the household of faith. Christian believers who are part of the spiritual remnant will be as an expectant father who is ready and waiting for the time to arrive when he will rush his wife to the hospital where she will immediately be taken to the maternity ward and the attending physician will do what needs to be done to deliver the baby. I can tell you as a father, when your child is due, you want to have somebody there who is an expert on delivery and knows what he is doing. 'Panic' may be defined by an excited father who rushes his expectant wife to the hospital emergency ward only to find a sign on the emergency room door saying 'closed due Obstetrician convention'. It would seem downright strange if the Heavenly Father were to remove all the baby doctors for a 7 year heavenly convention immediately before the biggest and most significant baby boom in the history of the universe is just about to take place. It wouldn't make sense in the physical world, and it doesn't make sense spiritually world either.

Dan.11:31

And forces from him will arise, desecrate the sanctuary fortress, and do away with the regular sacrifice. And they will set up the abomination of desolation.

The presence of '**they**' in this verse indicates it is more than just the action of one individual. It is also significant to note that 'they' do away with the '**regular**' sacrifice, that is, the grain offering. There isn't any mention of a blood sacrifice, which may be very important clue to the degree that the temple activity will be functionally restored immediately before the LORD'S return.

It is quite clear from such passages as Rev.13:5,6 and others, that Antichrist will over run Israel for 3 1/2 years, which will no doubt be the last half of the trib. period. The significance of this is that the 'Abomination of Desolation' occurs at the end of the tribulation, not the middle.

Dan.12:11

And from the time that the regular sacrifice is abolished, and the abomination of desolation is set up, there will be 1290 days.

I think the 1290 days is the span between the abolishment of the sacrifice and the abomination, not that the abolishment and the abomination are different terms for the same event. This is significant because, it indicates the exact number of days from the time of the abolishment of the grain offering to the end of the tribulation period of time, which will be identified by the abomination of desolation. The 45 days succeeding that event (Dan.12:12), could well be the length of time that will be used for a 'mop up' campaign by the LORD, and will culminate in the wedding feast.

DANIEL 9:26,27

> *Then after the sixty-two weeks the Messiah will be cut off and have nothing, and the people of the prince who is to come will destroy the city and the sanctuary. And its end will come with a flood; even to the end there will be war; desolations are determined. And he will make a firm covenant with the many for one week, but in the middle of the week he will put a stop to sacrifice and grain offering; and on the wing of abominations will come one who makes desolate, even until a complete destruction, one that is decreed, is poured out on the one who makes desolate.*

A point that should be noted in this verse, is the reference to 'the people' of the prince who is to come. If we assume that the prince who is to come is indeed the antichrist, then the people who destroyed the temple are the same nationality as he is. In other words, if we could identify the nationality of the people who destroyed the temple, we would also have the identity of the nationality of the antichrist. We don't have very far to look to determine that it was the Romans that destroyed the temple in 70ad, and it would then be a forgone conclusion that the coming antichrist would be 'Roman'. This point appears to have significant merit, and many have concluded this as incontrovertible indicator. There is another factor that goes un-noticed by most, but becomes glaringly apparent when one investigates the historical facts, and that is that there was also another nation that was instrumental in the fall of the temple and the fall of Jerusalem. The Idumea was a nation just to the south of Judea, and which had supplied even the likes of 'Herod' as procurator of Judea. The Idumeans gained access to the city of Jerusalem by promising to join forces against the common enemy Rome, but instead killed 8500 people inside the temple area, including the high priest 'Ananus'. They plundered every house and killed everyone they met with a degree of impiety that was considered as desecration. Josephus said that the death of Ananus by the Idumeans was the beginning of the destruction of Jerusalem[1], and that the Idumeans were a particularly barbarous and bloodthirsty people. Has Idumea ceased to exist, as the Bible dictionaries seem to imply? Does Idumea have a modern day equivalent? I don't know, but I am sure that there will be a nation existing in the last days that will have it's ancestry rooted in ancient Idumea, and it is to that nation that the LORD will personally go against with judgement and vengeance. Why would the LORD be so particularly vindictive against Idumea as Isaiah so graphically describes? Because of the 'sicari' or the actions of the Idumeans of around 70 AD? Perhaps, but I don't think so. I believe there is yet to come some kind of action by people half related to the Jews, that it becomes an abomination in the sight of the LORD to the point that they are exterminated and the nation becomes uninhabitable forever! Incidently, Idumea is also called Edom, Mt. Seir, Esau, and Bozrah, and to get the complete scenario you must examine what all the prophets have to say about all these different names.

The 'Abomination of Desolation' referred to in several passages of scripture has a 'proto-type' in an individual named Antiochus Epiphanies, or Antiochus IV the king of Syria at about the time 176-164 B.C. Antiochus apparently desecrated

---

[1] Josephus, *Wars of Jews*, Book iv, chap.v par.2.

the sacred temple more than one time, and the record of the things that he did should be noted, as the Antichrist of the last days will, I believe, do similar things. Moreover, it appears that of all the things that are ascribed to 'the despicable person' of Daniel 11:21 - 39 appear historically true of Antiochus IV. The Apocryphal books of 1 and 2 Maccabees are generally thought to be accurate historically, and while they aren't canonical by the reckoning of even Jerome, they do provide historical information that is important to the understanding of this most significant event. Many times Bible prophecy will have several 'types' that fulfill the prophecy, at least to a degree. In the case of the 'Abomination of Desolation' there are at least 2 figures that are 'types' of the antichrist's fulfillment during the final 'tribulation period'.

Antics of Antiochus

1. 'Antiochus dared to enter the most holy temple in all the world, guided by Menelaus, who had become a traitor both to the laws and to his country.'[2]

2. 'He took the holy vessels with his polluted hands,..'

3. 'So Antiochus carried off eighteen hundred talents from the temple,...' 'In his malice toward the Jewish citizens, Antiochus sent Apollonius, the captain of the Mysians, with an army of twenty-two thousand, and commanded him to slay all the grown men and to sell the women and boys as slaves'

4. He made an order for the 'Jews to forsake the laws of their fathers and cease to live by the laws of God, and also to pollute the temple in Jerusalem and call it the temple of Olympian Zeus, and to call the one in Gerizim the temple of Zeus the Friend of Strangers, as did the people who dwelt in that place.'

5. He 'had intercourse with women within the sacred pre-

---

[2] 2 Maccabees 6, *Oxford Apocrypha*, pg.272

cincts..'

6. 'The altar was covered with abominable offerings which were forbidden by the laws.'

7. 'A man could neither keep the sabbath, nor observe the feasts of his fathers, nor so much as confess himself to be a Jew.'

Other things too gross to relate are also mentioned in this book of 2 Maccabees chapter 6.

In an endeavour to obliterate Judaism and to bring Palestine under the influence of Hellenic culture, Antiochus ordered the cessation of sacrifices and of the observance of sabbaths, festivals and ceremonial regulations, prohibited the rite of circumcision, and destroyed the copies of the Scriptures, replaced the Feast of Tabernacles by a feast of Bacchus, introduced lewd practices among the youth of the city, and dedicated the temple to Jupiter Olympus. A heathen altar was erected upon the altar of burnt offering and for over three years the temple services were suspended. Many faithful Jews suffered because of their refusal to eat unclean meats or to defile themselves by obedience to the royal decree. Some were tortured or flogged and others even put to death. By such completely ruthless methods, it was hoped to obliterate Judaism and to supersede it by Hellenism.[3]

The title 'Epiphanies' is an abbreviation of 'theos epiphanies', which is the designation that Antiochus IV gave to himself. It is stamped on his coins, and means "the god who appears or reveals himself."[4] It is one of the same Greek words that is used to describe the second coming of the Lord Himself.

---

[3] Tatford, *The Climax of the Ages*, pg.198.

[4] I.S.B.E., vol.III, pg.1617.

Once a month a search was instituted, and whoever had possession of a copy of the Law or had observed the rite of c-ircumcision was condemned to death. In Jerusalem on the 15th of Chislev of the year 145, i.e. in December 168 BC, a pagan altar was built on the 'Great Altar of Burnt Sacrifices', and on the 25th of Chislev, sacrifice was brought on this altar for the first time(IMacc 1 54.59). This evidently was the"abomination of desolation." [5]

It seems quite clear that the reference in Daniel is fulfilled, by Antiochus IV, as the timing seems the same. Daniel 9:27 says that after 3 1/2 years the Antichrist will put a stop to the sacrifice and grain offering, after first making a 7 year pact with the Jews. Antiochus IV desecrated the temple for 3 1/2 years, which adds credulity to his prototype image. Josephus gives us this picture:

He also spoiled the temple, and put a stop to the constant practice of offering a daily sacrifice of expiation for three years and six months.'[6]

Many times Bible prophecy will have several 'types' that fulfill the prophecy,at least to a degree. In the case of the 'Abomination of Desolation' I find that there are at least 2 figures that are 'types' of the antichrist's fulfillment during the final 'tribulation period'. The first one, Antiochus IV, we have discussed, and the second was 'Titus'. I don't believe that Antiochus, in spite of is debauchery and despicable actions, totally destroyed the temple or the city of Jerusalem. We do find that in 70 AD that Titus, the commander of the Roman Army, did destroy the city and the temple in a terrible carnage. "Vespasian commenced the conquest in the north, and advanced by slow and certain steps. Being recalled to Rome as emperor in the midst of the war, the work of besieging and

---

[5] I Maccabees 1:20-23, *The Oxford Annotated Apocrypha.*

[6] Josephus,*Wars of the Jews,* pg.429

capturing the city itself fell to his son Titus. None of the many calamities which had happened to the city are to be compared with this terrible siege. In none had the city been so magnificent, its fortifications so powerful, its population so crowded. It was Passover time, but, in addition to the crowds assembled for this event, vast numbers had hurried there, flying from the advancing Roman army. The loss of life was enormous; refugees to Titus gave 600,000 as the number dead, but this seems incredible."[7]

Josephus writes about this terrible day of destruction:
"On the 105th day - the ominous 9th of AB - the temple and the lower city were burnt, and the last day found the whole city in flames. "..the rest of the city was dug up to its foundations.[8]
As to the number of casualties, Flavius Josephus records an incredible number, which many believe to be an exaggeration.

"Now the number of those that were carried captive during this whole war was collected to be ninety-seven thousand; as was the number of those that perished during the whole siege, eleven hundred thousand,[9]

The Ninth of AV

One of the unique things that I discovered when researching this project was something called the 'Fast of Tishah' as found

---

[7] I.S.B.E., pg. 1619.

[8] Josephus, ibid. book V, pg. 587.

[9] Josephus, ibid.

in (Zech.8:19), according to the Jewish Directory[10].

Zech.8:19

Thus says the LORD of hosts, 'The fast of the fourth, and the fast of the fifth, the fast of the seventh, and the fast of the tenth months will become joy, gladness, and cheerful feasts for the house of Judah, so love truth and peace.'

In reality, the date has been pock marked with disaster, grief, tears, bloodshed, humiliation, and national disgrace. It became a time for sackcloth and ashes, not joy, gladness, and cheer. Here are a few of the reasons cited form the Jewish Directory that reflect the grief of the occasion. In each example, the date fell on the Jewish calender date of AV 9, which apparently was on the day that the feast of the tenth month was to take place.

* The Exodus generation was condemned to die in the desert (Deut.1:35).
* Nebuchadnezzar set fire to the Temple 586 BCE
* The Romans destroyed the Second Temple on August 29, 70 CE.
* Betar the last independent outpost under Bar Kochba, fell to the Romans on Aug 5, 135.
* King Edward I of England ordered the expulsion of all Jews on July 18, 1290.
* The period of expulsion of the Jews from Spain commenced on Aug 2, 1492.
* World War I broke out on Aug 1, 1914.

It would not surprise me if AV 9 fell exactly 3 1/2 years

---

10 *The 1986 Jewish Directory and Almanac*, Pacific Press.

from the middle of the tribulation period, when Antichrist will commit the 'abomination of desolation', and the ultimate 'low' of Jewish history will occur.

8.
MYSTERY OF CHRIST

It may well be that the complete understanding of prophecy relating to the rapture is rooted deeply in Ecclesiology rather than Eschatology itself, and the understanding of what the 'church' really **is** may well be significant to the understanding of what the 'rapture' really is.

Many evangelicals accept a definition of the 'church' as the body of Christ that began at pentecost and ends at the rapture, and while it may be convenient to dispensationally categorize that way, its etymology becomes crowded. The word 'church'[1] has a much broader scope than that which we are accustomed to use, and includes 1.) 'assembly' as a regularly summoned political body; 2.) 'assemblage, gathering, meeting' in general; 3.) the 'congregation of the Israelites'; 4.) the 'christian church or congregation'.[2] I believe most evangelicals today are relatively cognizant of the church as being the body of Christ that assembles in a regular manner at a specific location and have some type of organizational structure. The common orthodox use of the term, unfortunately, is in reference to a denomination, or to a building that represents an organized denomination or group.

---

[1] εκκλησια

[2] Arndt and Gingrich. p.240.

The church was not started in a 'twinkling of an eye'. It took a period of time between the ascension and pentecost for the body to be born and to begin to function, and it may take some time for it to come to fruition at the final end as well.

Abraham is considered the father of three major religions in the world today: Judaism, Christianity, and Islam. He was the father of all who 'believe' even before circumcision became the symbol of believing Jewish heritage, and as such becomes the forerunner of all who believe by 'faith' (Rom 4:11). Paul lays a foundation of 'faith' rather than 'heritage' as a condition of acceptance into the household of faith, and that is not to suggest a dissolving of Israel, or that the Church supports the status of Israel as the object of the promises and covenants of God. (Rom.9:3-8).

Rom.2:28,29

> *For he is not a Jew who is one outwardly; neither is circumcision that which is outward in the flesh; but he is a Jew who is one inwardly' and circumcision is that which is of the heart, by the Spirit, not by the letter; and his praise is not from men, but from God.*

We used to sing a little chorus in sunday school, " ...every promise in the book is mine, every chapter, every verse, every line...". The melody is great, and the chorus inspiring, but the theology is incorrect as far as I can determine, because there are promises in the bible that really aren't for the 'church' at all. What am I trying to say? Its obvious from the text just quoted that a believer is to be considered a 'spiritual jew', right? Well...not quite. Paul was speaking of 'natural' jews that became believers, not gentiles that became 'spiritual' jews. There is something special about that nationality that can't be absolved, dissolved, or resolved by either force or faith until Messiah reclaims them nationally.

The question "What is the church?", is somewhat more profound than we might first imagine. There is almost a reversal of roles in the history of the church today, where the church has assumed the attitudes of some of the pre church jewish sects. Some of us have become cocky in our position of favor with the Lord, and have forgotten what we really are and where we really came from. Many of us have associated the 'church' as the 'bride of Christ' that will be removed by the bridegroom immediately before the tribulation begins, in which the 'unsaved jews' will be dealt with by God Himself through judgement and affliction until they finally come around to accepting Him as Messiah. What we have done, in effect, is to subjugate Israel into an almost non existent relationship with God, while we, the gentile church, are feasting at the marriage supper of the Lamb.

God has not, in fact, rejected His people whom he foreknew (Rom.11:2), but is using the believing gentiles to make them jealous (Rom.11:11). As a natural branch is broken off and a wild olive is grafted in, so the Gentile believer partakes in the kingdom of God (Rom.11:17). Many people will come from the east and the west, and recline at table with Abraham, and Isaac, and Jacob, in the kingdom of heaven; but the sons of the kingdom shall be cast out (Mt.8:11,12). The sons of the kingdom that are cast out are the natural born Jews who really could have inherited the kingdom spiritually but chose not to, and the foreigners, i.e. gentile believers, will have communion with the saints of old in the kingdom of heaven.

Jesus said 'I desire compassion and not sacrifice' because he came 'not to call the righteous, but sinners' (Mt.9:13). The typical religious Jew during the days of Christ was so very religious, that he missed the whole point of what the sacrifices he was performing in the temple were intended to do.

The whole concept of 'church' was not intended to be like 'Listerene antiseptic' or a 'Johnson and Johnson bandaid' placed over an infected sore by the great physician. It was not intended as a quick 'iron-on' patch placed on frayed threads of a hole worn through the knee of a pair of threadbear jeans (Mt.9:16). I think we understand that concept fine, but the problem is that we have also taken the position of the very people we have replaced. We have unconsciously often assumed the role of the self righteous Pharisees of Israel that is now self righteous about the position in the Church, and mutually exclusive of all else. Here are a just a few similarities that I have observed:

The Pharisees:

* '...tie up heavy loads and lay them on mens shoulders...'-(Mt.23:4);
* '...do all their deeds to be noticed by men...'(Mt.23:5);
* '...love the place of honor at banquets and chief seats in the synagogues', and love being called 'rabbi' by men-(Mt.23:7);

The Church:

* makes rules about what is proper for a christian to do and not to do, which often border on legalism, that is, making a rules for someone else to follow;
* makes sure the rest of the world knows that they are 'christians' and that the rest of the world is going to hell;
* has leaders with several adjectives in front of their names and several initials after it.

Nearly everyone is familiar with the parable of the prodigal son of Luke 15, where the younger son requested his inheritance early, and squandered it on 'loose living', and then after much humiliation, returned home, and was met by the father who had a feast in his honor. I suppose there are a lot of analogues that can be drawn from this parable, and one of the most common is to associate Israel with the older son and the Gentiles as the younger son that was lost. Suppose for a moment that the situation is reversed. The younger son is Israel and the older son is the Church today, that has been with the Father for nearly 2000 years, and has 'an attitude problem' in that he is not willing to receive the younger son back into the fold again. We know from the scripture that

Israel is going to come into God's household again, but we have already relegated them to a lesser position within the family of God. They are the 'friend of the bridegroom', while we as the gentile church, are the 'bride'. The father didn't approve of his younger son living away from home and in sin, but when the younger son returned home, the father received him with rejoicing. Now if the father knew ahead of time that the younger son was returning home, would he not make the older son wait for him too? The church today doesn't want to wait for the younger son. The church wants to leave immediately, and let the younger son fend for himself in the time of his dire humiliation. I know, I'm presupposing they have equal relationship with the father, and I'll get to that later.

I cannot help but imagine the passion of Jesus as he nears the end of His ministry shortly before the time of the crucifixion and looks over the holy city and exclaims:

Mat.23:37

> *O Jerusalem, Jerusalem, who kills the prophets and stones those who are sent to her! How often I wanted to gather your children together, the way a hen gathers her chicks under her wings, and you were unwilling.*

and later as He entered Jerusalem on the back of the donkey on the day we call 'Palm Sunday', He saw the city and 'wept over it'(Lk.19:41) because they did not recognize the 'time of your visitation' (Lk.19:44).

The church council

When the church began, it consisted only of Jews! Jesus, the 12 apostles, the 120 in the upper room, the 3000, then the 5000 in Jerusalem, etc. It wasn't until Acts 10 when Cornelius the gentile became a christian that the message of the gospel was even open to anyone that wasn't Jewish. Some of the more traditional Jews thought that anyone becoming a follower of Jesus and receiving the Holy Spirit must also become a Jew and be circumcised. Acts 15 is a record of the first church council at Jerusalem which met to determine if people who became believers had to also become Jewish or not. The church council decided that they should lay no additional burden upon the recent gentile converts except that they abstain from things sacrificed to idols, blood, things strangled, and fornication. (Acts 15:28,29). I bring this up, because today the church is nearly all gentile with only a small representation of Jewish believers. Historically, the church, especially the Roman Catholic Church has not looked very favorably upon Jews, and in fact some of the church history during the dark ages is so detestable, and reprobate that some have concluded that the Papacy was the fulfillment of the prophecies regarding Babylon of (Rev.17)[3] Since 1948 when Israel became a nation, Israel has taken on a new significance, and a resurgence of the study of biblical prophecy has engendered numerous books about the Middle East. It is my opinion that the attitude of the church as a whole has changed with respect to its acceptance of Christian Jews, but this has not always been the case. The church today is primarily gentile, and the attitude toward the Jew is one of sadness for the trial she went through during the second world war, and one of sympathy for the Nation surrounded by hostile Arabs that outnumber her ten to one. But, in spite of the sympathy, the church (as a whole) is nearly ignorant of the spiritual relationship that it has with Israel, and this is most unfortunate because the Lord is doing something in our day that we don't understand.

The Mystery of Christ

The apostle Paul wrote about the 'mystery of Christ'(Eph.3:4), and relates that it was given to other generations but has now been revealed to his Holy apostles and prophets in the Spirit; that the gentiles are "...fellow heirs and fellow members of the body, and fellow partakers of the promise in Christ Jesus

---

[3] Hislop, *The Two Babylons*.

through the gospel..."(Eph.3:6). The gentiles formerly were "excluded from the commonwealth of Israel ", strangers to the promise and without God.(Eph.2:11,12), but God saw fit to include the gentiles by breaking down the barriers between the two and creating "one new man"(Eph 2:15). It is by the Spirit that we "both have our access" to the Father and we are "fellow citizens" with the "saints", and part of God's household. This is compared to a temple building in which the apostles and prophets are foundation stones and Jesus is the chief cornerstone. This building is fitted "together" and makes a dwelling place of God in the Spirit. As I was doing this study I noticed several different terms are used by Paul in his epistles to describe this union of Jew and Gentile, and I have listed a few:

Commonwealth of Israel (Eph.2:12)
one new man (Eph.2:15)
one body (Rom 12:5)
fellow citizens (Eph.2:19)
fellow heirs (Eph.3:6)
fellow members (Eph.3:6)
fellow partakers(Eph.3:6)
God's household (Eph.2:19)
God's field (1Cor.3:9)
God's building (1Cor.3:9)
a holy temple (Eph.2:21)
a dwelling of God (Eph.2:22)
church (Eph.1:22)
a building (Eph.2:21)
a mature man (Eph.4:13)
the whole body (Eph.4:16)
the body of Christ (Eph.4:12)
His body (Eph.1:23)
sons of Abraham (Gal.3:7)
sons of God (Gal.3:26)
Abraham's offspring (Gal.3:29)
heirs according to the promise (Gal.3:29)

sons of God (Gal.4:6)(Rom.8:14)
children of God.(Rom.8:16)
a new creation (Gal.6:15)
the Israel of God (Gal 6:16)
descendants of Abraham (Rom.4:16)
heirs of God (Rom.8:17)
the olive tree (Rom.11)
the temple of the living God. (2Cor.6:16)

Gal.3:28,29

There is neither Jew nor Greek, there is neither slave nor free man, there is neither male nor female; for you are all one in Christ Jesus.

And if you belong to Christ, then you are Abraham's offspring, heirs according to promise.

Rom.9:6,7,8

But it is not as though the word of God has failed. For they are not all Israel who are descended from Israel;

neither are they all children because they are Abraham's descendants, but: "through Isaac your descendants will be named."

That is, it is not the children of the flesh who are children of God, but the children of the promise are regarded as descendants.

Just because a person is born Jewish, does not automatically make him a true descendant of Abraham, and not only that, not everybody that is a descendant of Abraham is Jewish! It sounds a little confusing at first, but if you think about it for a second, it makes sense.

Rom.9:24,25,26

even us, whom He also called, not from among

Jews only, but also from among Gentiles.
As He says also in Hosea, "I will call those who were not My people, My people, and her who was not beloved, 'beloved'"
"And it shall be that in the place were it was said to them 'you are not my people', there they shall be called sons of the living God"

Notice that Paul refers to the passage in (Hosea 1:10), which was the place specified where God said they were not His people, which was actually the name of Hosea's son (Lo-ammi) who was a living, graphic, audio-visual aid. The second part of the quote from Hos 2:23, where God says 'You are My people' - from the context of Hosea, happens (guess when?) - on 'that day' at the consummation of the battle of Armageddon in the valley of Jezreel. Do you see the point here? Paul is using the very same text that God has given to Israel unto the climax of the ages when He will become their Messiah, and they will become His people - to **us** the Gentiles, right now! The relationship between Israel and the Church is incontrovertible!!

In Romans 11, Paul uses the illustration of the olive tree that had some of the natural branches broken off, and some wild olive branches grafted in, and he uses that as an illustration of the gentiles who have been brought into the family of God and grafted into the mainstream, while the natural branches have been cut off. He goes on to exhort the wild olive branches (the gentile church) not to get conceited, but to recognize that the wild olive branch can be broken off in the same way that the natural branch was broken off. The natural branch that was broken off can again be grafted into the mainstream of the olive tree, because God is able to do just that. If we (gentiles) as a wild olive branch are grafted in, how much more can the natural branches be grafted into their own tree? And when are they going to be grafted into the olive tree? - When the fullness of the Gentiles has come in, and all Israel will be saved.(Rom.11:25).

The Lord's Prayer

John 17:11

And I am no more in the world; and yet they themselves are in the world, and I come to Thee. Holy Father, keep them in Thy name, the name which Thou hast given Me, that they may be one, even as We are.

John 17:21

that they may all be one; even as Thou, Father, art in Me, and I in Thee, that they also may be in Us; that the world may believe that Thou didst send Me.

John 17:23

I in them, and Thou in Me, that they may be perfected in unity, that the world may know that Thou didst send Me, and didst love the, even as Thou didst love Me.

The 17th chapter of John is what some of us call the 'Lord's prayer', and in it, Jesus prays 3 times to the Father concerning the **unity** of His disciples. I guess I have always associated this prayer with the concept that the Christians need to get their act together today, and join forces. Baptist and Lutheran, Catholic and Methodist, all different Christian religions need to put away their prejudices and feelings, and all join hands and form a daisy chain across America in sympathy of aids victims. Of course I'm being factious and cynical, and of course, there shouldn't be divisions among the brethren either. I really don't think that Jesus is referring to this kind of unity either though, because even the world forms daisy chains for causes that they think are worthy of unity, so how would the world be impressed with that? Jesus said that the world would hate them, but that because of the unity, the world would know, and believe that Jesus is the 'sent one' from the Father.

I think Diedrich Bonhoffer might have a different interpretation of this passage than the church does today. I think Jesus had something deeper in mind than Baptists going to a Methodist pancake breakfast, or Presbyterians going to an Episcopal Lenten service. I think He is talking about the divisions that occur between Jew and Gentile christians, which did occur shortly after the church was born, and which still continues in some measure today. It was the cause of the first church council in Jerusalem in Acts 15, and I believe the Lord's prayer was answered there. The thing is though, that this isn't over with yet. There is still a large portion of believers to be added to the church, and I believe that Jesus prayer is still to be considered 'effectual' in the bringing together the last great 'in gathering' into the church, and guess what? The church doesn't want any part of it! No! I'm not kidding here folks. the church is ready to pack it in and move out right now in anticipation of a pretrib rapture that would leave behind a whole nation of Jews that haven't become believers yet, because the eyes of their understanding is temporarily blinded until Jesus returns at the end of the tribulation.

Do you understand the significance of this? Israel has been temporarily blinded in their recognition of Messiah, and the gentile church has been temporarily blinded concerning Israel. We have been given insight into the 'mystery of Christ' by the Apostle Paul, but that insight is contingent upon how much light we let in. As gentiles, our understanding was formerly in spiritual darkness (Eph.4:17,), and we are exhorted to walk as children of light (Eph.5:8), and to wake up from our darkness (Eph.5:14). We like to visualize ourselves as spiritual giants because we have the Holy Spirit and gifts, but we too quickly forget that we were delivered from a 'domain of darkness' (Col.1:13) that we were once part of, and that the church is a 'mystery' (Col.1:26,27) that has been 'hidden' but is now revealed! We would like to believe that as soon as we become believers, we instantly understand all these mysteries, but it really is an unveiling process and takes some time. I have often heard Christian's make reference to the church today as the 'Laodicean' church, which presupposes a lot of theological implications, but which may well have some merit in its interpretation from Revelation. One of the things that characterized the Laodicean church was blindness,...but of course the blindness refers to the sinful ubiquitous 'them' never the repentant, spiritual 'us'.

9.

BABYLON THE GREAT

Lam.1:1,2

How lonely sits the city that was full of people! She has become like a widow who was once great among the nations! She who was a princess among the provinces has become a forced laborer! She weeps bitterly in the night, and her tears are on her cheeks; She has none to comfort her among all her lovers. All her friends have dealt treacherously with her; They have become her enemies.

Rev. 17:5

and upon her forehead a name was written, a mystery, "BABYLON THE GREAT, THE MOTHER OF HARLOTS AND OF THE ABOMINATIONS OF THE EARTH."

called a mystery

Every so often in the scriptures, we come across a subject that is called a 'mystery'. A 'mystery' in the scriptures is not like a drugstore paperback novel that has to do with an unsolved crime, but is something that is intentionally difficult to understand, but which can be deciphered with some investigation. It does not mean that the topic is totally beyond the understanding, and often it is a topic that is being revealed at the time of the writing, that was not previously understood. There are at least 11 'mysteries' in the scriptures, and many of them are directly related to biblical prophecy, such as the mystery of the translation (rapture) (1 Cor.15:51); the mystery of the Jew and Gentile in the Church, which is called 'the mystery of Christ'(Eph.3:4); and the 'mystery of lawlessness' (2 Thes.2:7). Some 'mysteries' are revealed directly in the text they are described in, and others are a bit more enigmatic and require some investigation to determine correctly. Babylon has been an object of much conjecture by bible scholars over the years, and many different interpretations have ensued to explain its mystery. Many books written on the topic have arrived at widely variant conclusions, such as "The Two Babylons"[1] which describe in very exacting details the relationship of ancient Babylon with the Papal worship of the Roman Catholic Church. This very involved and detailed work examines the archeological evidences that support the conversion of paganism to the Papal system, and is extremely scholarly in its content, and anyone reading the book would need to be quite well read in archaeology to even evaluate the information displayed. Another book, "America and After in Prophecy"[2] investigates some rather obscure facts about America, such as the 'seals' of the state of New York, the Federal Trade Commission and the U.S.Dollar; the emblems of the United Nations, and Russia; and facts about the monetary system and the United Nations organization, and concludes that 'America' is the 'Babylon' spoken of in Biblical prophecy. Both of these books support some legitimate and scholarly analysis of little known facts, but they arrive at totally different conclusions. In examining the other 'mysteries' of the Bible, we find that the key to the mystery is

---

[1] Alexander Hislop, *The Two Babylons*

[2] Raymond Thomas, *America and After in Prophecy.*

found within the confines of the scriptures themselves, and don't require enigmatic enlightenment in little known historical or archaeological facts. It seems logical to me that the unlocking of the 'mystery of Babylon' could also be determined by a careful investigation of scripture itself without involving external deciphering of obscure historical, political, or archaeological information. With this thought in mind, I have searched through the scriptures looking for clues as to the identity of this mystery, and have determined to my satisfaction, its identity.

The historical Babylon

The assumption is often made that because Babylon is spoken of as a mystery, that it is figurative and not literal. Literal Babylon was a city kingdom in Mesopotamia where civilization had its conception, alongside the Euphrates River, that is now inside the borders of the current nation of Iraq, 54 miles south of the modern city of Baghdad. Babylon began as a result of Nimrod, the son of Cush, a Hamite (Gen.10:8,9,10), who began the city of 'Babel', or 'Babylon', in the land of Shinar. The people all spoke the same words and the same language (Gen.11:1), and decided to build a tower, "...whose top will reach into heaven..."(Gen.11:4). The Lord observed the tower, and confounded the language so that they all spoke different words, and because of it the tower was called 'Babel'(Gen.11:9). The city became famous for the splendor of its hanging gardens and was considered one of the 7 wonders of the ancient world. It reached a pinnacle of importance and prominence during the time of Nebuchadnezzar II (605-562 B.C.), who build "...Babylon the great..."as a 'royal residence' for the glory of his majesty (Dan.4:30). Records of this great city can be seen through the artifacts that remain to tell about its glory such as the famed

Gate of Ishtar.[3] Babylon is closely associated with Assyria, and indeed, both were founded by Nimrod (Gen.10:11). The history of these nations rise somewhat simultaneously, and the dominant nation went back and forth several times during the course of their history. Cyrus of Persia conquered Babylon in 539 BC, and Babylon was under the Achemedid rule until Alexander the Great defeated Persia (331 BC), and after his death, Babylon was neglected and eventually abandoned. Extensive excavations have been done on the city by many archaeologists who have unearthed many things, but it remains today an uninhabited ruin, fulfilling the prophecy that it would be "...an everlastingdesolation..."(Jer.25:12),"...desolateforever..."(Jer.51:26),"...a heap of ruins..."(Jer.51:37),"...nothing dwelling in it, whether man or beast, but it will be a perpetual desolation..."(Jer.51:62). From prophecies such as these, we can be pretty sure that Babylon, the historical city, will never be revived to fulfill the prophecies about Babylon of Revelation, which figures into the scheme of the end times. Babylon was of course already in ruins before John wrote Revelation, which also adds weight to the postulation that Babylon is a figurative reference. Many of the scriptural references to Babylon speak of the historical Babylon in an immediate prophecy, and a later fulfillment to a figurative Babylon during the last days,and this overlap of prophecy compounds the difficulty in understanding what is going to transpire in the future. Both cities were to be destroyed by a kingdom from the north, and we already know that literal Babylon was destroyed by the Persians, but is Persia the kingdom of the North that will destroy figurative Babylon?

Reasons for the destruction of Babylon

Jeremiah 50 and 51 give us a some reasons as to why the destruction took place, and since there is a correlation between the literal and the figurative, it may give us some clues as to

---

[3] Pfeiffer, *The Biblical World*, photo pg.130

its identity.

1.) Judgement because of the Lord's vengeance for His temple. (Jer.51:11)(Jer.50:28). This obviously is in reference to 606B.C. when Nebuchadnezzar sacked the temple, and carried away the gold items and some of the people to Babylon for 70 years. There is no central temple in Jerusalem at present, that would in any way compare to the temple that was destroyed by Babylon, but to allegorize the matter, it may figuratively apply to the spiritual temple today, which is the church, and/or God's people of spiritual Israel. This seems like a possibility based on the number of martyrs that occur during the tribulation period (Rev.6:9,10; Rev.20:4;).

2.) Judgement because of the slain of Israel(Jer.51:49)
Many nations have contributed greatly towards their own judgement in respect to their treatment of the Jews. Ancient nations of Babylon, Assyria, Rome, and modern nations like Germany, and Russia have filled their own cup with judgement. But America? Not unless it has a total reversal of policy toward Israel in the very near future. There are nearly as many Jews in America (3.5 million), as there are in Israel (4.2 million). America was the first nation to officially recognize the existence of Israel as a nation in 1948, and has been one of her only allies through the periods of her great stress with the arab countries that surround her. Financial support, military support, informational support and moral support have made America the best friend Israel has. If for no other reason that this argument alone, it would be enough to look elsewhere for figurative Babylon than America.

3.) Judgement "...because you have engaged in conflict with the LORD." (Jer.50:24).
Any conflict with the Lords people could be considered an open conflict with the Lord Himself. Any nation that has openly engaged in warfare with Israel in times past could qualify for this judgement, but it does preclude America, since it never has engaged in conflict with Israel or directly opposed the

Lord. Quite the contrary, America has supported more missionaries than the rest of the nations put together, and it has since its inception, been a refuge for people religiously oppressed, who wanted to be able to worship God without persecution.

4.) Judgement will be because of the treatment she has done to others. "...as she has done to others, so do to her." (Jer.50:-15). Again, America fails to meet the qualifications here, because of the aid she has given to people desperate from national calamities, war, earthquakes, famines, floods, etc. While it is so that the Roman Church persecuted people during the dark ages, it isn't generally characteristic of her attitude either.

5.) "...Repay her according to her work..." (Jer.50:29)
Whatever deeds Babylon has done, she is going to be judged by them, and rewarded accordingly.

6.) Judgement because "...she has become arrogant against the LORD..." (Jer.50:29).
Both the Catholic Church and America are guilty on this point, but to what extent? America has made itself a god of immorality, drugs, and violence. She has taken into her own hands the souls of millions of unborn children through abortion. She has taken ethics into her own hands by saying wrong is right.

There may be many more reasons why judgement will be meted out to Babylon, but these at least, demonstrate why neither America nor the Catholic Church could figuratively be considered Babylon. It nonetheless does not preclude that both could be judged, and undoubtedly will be, but not as a symbolic Babylon.

Significant facts about Babylon

1.) It is significant enough that an angel is given the specific task of declaring its demise.

(Rev.14:8)

> *And another angel, a second one, followed, saying "fallen, fallen is Babylon the great, she who has made all the nations drink of the wine of the passion of her immorality."*

2.) It is called "the great". (Rev.14:8).
This indicates that there is some fame connected with it that is unusual.

3.) She is considered immoral. (Rev.14:8).
We will assume that the Lord is speaking here of spiritual immorality, which would be to include another god besides Himself.

4.) It is specifically called a city.

> (Rev.16:19)
> *And the great city was split into three parts, and the cities of the nations fell. And Babylon the great was remembered before God, to give her the cup of the wine of His fierce wrath.*

5.) The city is split into three parts. (Rev.16:19).

6.) It is judged by God in His fierce wrath. (Rev.16:19).

7.) It is remembered before God. (Rev.16:19).
This seems almost in contrast to sin confessed to God and forgotten. Here, the sin is not confessed, and remembered.

8.) It is called "...the great harlot..." (Rev.17:1).

9.) She sits on "...many waters..."(Rev.17:1)
This probably indicates authority over people, since waters indicate the populace as revealed in (Rev.17:15).

10.) Kings and those of earth have become drunk with the wine of her immorality. (Rev.17:2).

11.) she is a woman (Rev.17:3).

12.) she sits on a scarlet beast.(Rev.17:3).
This beast has 7 heads and 10 horns, and undoubtedly is the 10

kingdom nation that comes to power in the last days before the Lord personally brings condemnation and judgement.

13.) She is clothed in purple and scarlet.(Rev.17:4)
I have thought that because the Roman Catholic priests, bishops, cardinals, and popes have all these opulent rich robes, that this may pertain to Rome, but it could be just an indication that this city reflects a quality of splendor that adorns royalty.

14.) She is adorned with gold, precious stones and pearls (Rev.17:4). Her attire is that of extreme wealth, and she is dressed to the hilt. Nothing is too good for her taste.

15.) She has a cup of abominations in her hand (Rev.17:4)
The cup is a symbol of something that must be consumed by the one that holds the cup. Jesus spoke of the cup He had to drink and Paul spoke of a cup of blessing, but most of the examples in scripture are in conjunction with judgement.

16.) She is called the "mother of harlots" (Rev.17:5).

17.) She is drunk with the blood of saints.(Rev.17:6).
This is a key verse, because it says that in this city, saints were killed. Saints here most likely means spiritual sons of Abraham.

18.) She is also drunk with the blood of the witnesses of Jesus. (Rev.17:6).

19.) Babylon is going to be destroyed and plundered by the ten kingdom empire of the antichrist, and then burned with fire. (Rev.17:16).

20.) It is "...the great city which reigns over the kings of the earth." (Rev.17:18).
Those who support the concept that Rome is Babylon, would undoubtedly claim this verse substantiates their claim, because Rome has indeed ruled over kings. More significantly, though,

is what the last part of this verse says in Greek.[4] Basilica (kingdom) is the english word that is derived from word translated as 'reigns'. Literally it is a kingdom over the kings of the earth. There is a play on words here, which would have some significance if the kingdom was 'The Vatican City'.

21.) God's people are told to abandon the city (Rev.18:4)
In order that the plagues that are going to be sent upon the city doesn't affect the true sons of God, God gives them a warning to flee the city before the destruction comes upon it.

22.) Her sin has piled up as high as heaven (Rev.18:5).
The evil that this city has committed is extremely offensive to God.

23.) She said in her heart, "I sit as a queen and I am not a widow, and I will never see mourning" (Rev.18:7)
There is an arrogance of royalty about this city, that says she is not a widow.

24.) The Lord judges her in one day with pestilence, mourning, famine, and fire. (Rev.18:8).

25.) Merchants will lament at a distance at the smoke of her burning. (Rev. 18:10).

26.) The city is involved intrinsically with commerce and shipping of jewelry, cloth, wood, stone, metals, food, meat, automobiles, and slaves. (Rev. 18:12,13).
Those that claim America is Babylon will undoubtedly claim this verse reflects the current trend, where the USA is the market place for the rest of the worlds commodities.

27.) Those that make their living by the sea throw dust on their heads lamenting for the burning city. (Rev. 18:19).

28.) Saints, apostles, and prophets are told to rejoice, be-

---

[4] *βασιλειαν επι των βασιλεων*

cause God has pronounced judgement against the city. (Rev.18:-20).

29.) The voice of the bride and bridegroom will not be heard in her any longer.(Rev.18:23).
If the bride and bridegroom are allegorical in nature, then John is talking about Christ and the Church no longer being in the city.

30.) Her merchants were the great men of the earth.(Rev.18:-23).

31.) The blood of prophets, saints, and all who have been slain on earth were found in her. (Rev.18:24).
The people of God were martyred in this city, and the judgement upon her is representative of all the blood spilled by all who have ever been killed.

The solution to the mystery of Babylon

Have you guessed the identity yet? One of the keys to understanding its identity is item 31. The blood of saints has been found in many cities, Rome included, but when did Rome kill the prophets of Israel? Jesus tells us:

Mat.23:37

> *O Jerusalem, Jerusalem, who kills the prophets and stones those who are sent to her!..."*

Mat.23:35

> *that upon you may fall the guilt of all the righteous blood shed on earth, from the blood or righteous Abel to the blood of Zechariah, the son of Berechiah, whom you murdered between the temple and the altar.*

That's right, Jerusalem is the identity of mystical Babylon. Jerusalem becomes the object of wrath of the Messiah, and when He judges it, he uses the city as a representative of all the innocent blood that has been shed. There is a striking parallel here, where Jesus takes upon Himself the sin of those who trust in Him, and Jerusalem receives the judgement of all those innocent people that have been slain.

Rev.11:8

> *and their dead bodies will lie in the street of the great city which mystically is called Sodom and Egypt, where also their Lord was crucified.*

The Lord was crucified Jerusalem, and that is the city were the two prophets will lie in the street. It is called the great city, and so is mystical Babylon. To be considered 'great' means that there is something significant about the city that no other city can claim. Jerusalem has to be the most different and unusual city in the entire world, for there the Lord was crucified, and there the church was born, and there was the temple was located. It is later called 'The Holy City' (Rev.21:2,10), but the 'holy city' is really a 'new Jerusalem' which comes down out of heaven, as a bride for her husband. We often refer to Jerusalem as 'The Holy City' without really realizing that the Jerusalem we normally refer to is not the same as the 'New Jerusalem' at all, but is spiritually called 'Babylon', 'Sodom', and 'Egypt'.

It has a mystical name of Sodom and Egypt, which establishes precedence for other mystical names for the city as well. Sodom speaks of immorality, and Egypt worldliness.

Jer.4:30

> *And you, O desolate one, what will you do? Although you dress in scarlet, Although you decorate yourself with ornaments of gold, Although you enlarge your eyes with paint, in vain you make yourself beautiful; Your lovers despise you; They seek your life.*

We have already seen that Babylon was to be desolate, and that she was dressed in scarlet (see item 13), and that she was dressed in gold (see item 14), and that she had lovers (see item

3), and that her lovers despised her (see item 19).

Isa.3:8,9

For Jerusalem has stumbled, and Judah has fallen, Because their speech and their actions are against the LORD, To rebel against His glorious presence, The expression of their faces bears witness against them. And they display their sin like Sodom; They do not even conceal it. Woe to Them! For they have brought evil on themselves.

Here is the reason why Jerusalem is called Sodom in the book of Revelation, because they are not ashamed of their sins, and don't even try to conceal it. In this respect America could also be called 'Sodom' for the way the homosexuals and libertines have flaunted their sin. America deserves judgement, and like Bob Harrington used to say, "If God doesn't judge America, He will have to apologize to Sodom and Gomorrah."

Isa.4:4

When the LORD has washed away the filth of the daughters of Zion, and purged the bloodshed of Jerusalem from her midst, by the spirit of judgement and the spirit of burning,

Compare this verse with (item 18) for the judgement due to bloodshed; and (see item 19) where Babylon is going to be burned with fire; and (see item 24) where the Lord is the one that does the judging.

Isa 47:1

Come down and sit in the dust, O virgin daughter of Babylon;..."

From the context, it is obvious that it is not Babylon that is being called the daughter of Babylon, but Israel that was taken captive in Babylon for 70 years.

Isa.47:3 "...your nakedness will be exposed..."

Isa.47:3 "...I will take vengeance..." (see item 24)

Isa 47:5 "...you will no longer be called The Queen of Kingdoms"; Isa 47:7; "Yet you said, I shall be a queen forever..."; Isa 47:8," I shall not sit as a widow; Nor shall I know loss of children"; Isa 47:9 "But these two things shall come on you suddenly in one day; Loss of children and widowhood..." (see item 23).

Luke 21:20,21

> *But when you see Jerusalem surrounded by armies, then recognize that her desolation is at hand. Then let those who are in Judea flee to the mountains, and let those who are in the midst of the city depart, and let not those who are in the country enter the city;*

Compare this to (item 21) from (Rev.18:4) where God's people are told to abandon the city before its judgement. This happened once before to Jerusalem (70 AD), and it will happen again to Jerusalem immediately before the destruction by the Antichrist during the tribulation.

We have examined the scripture pertaining to the facts about mystical Babylon of the last days, and demonstrated the same facts also pertain to Jerusalem, and must logically conclude that they are the same. While our scriptural research and logical conclusions dictate one thing, our emotions and instincts dictate quite the opposite, and thus (until further research discovers additional arguments), Babylon still remains 'a mystery'.

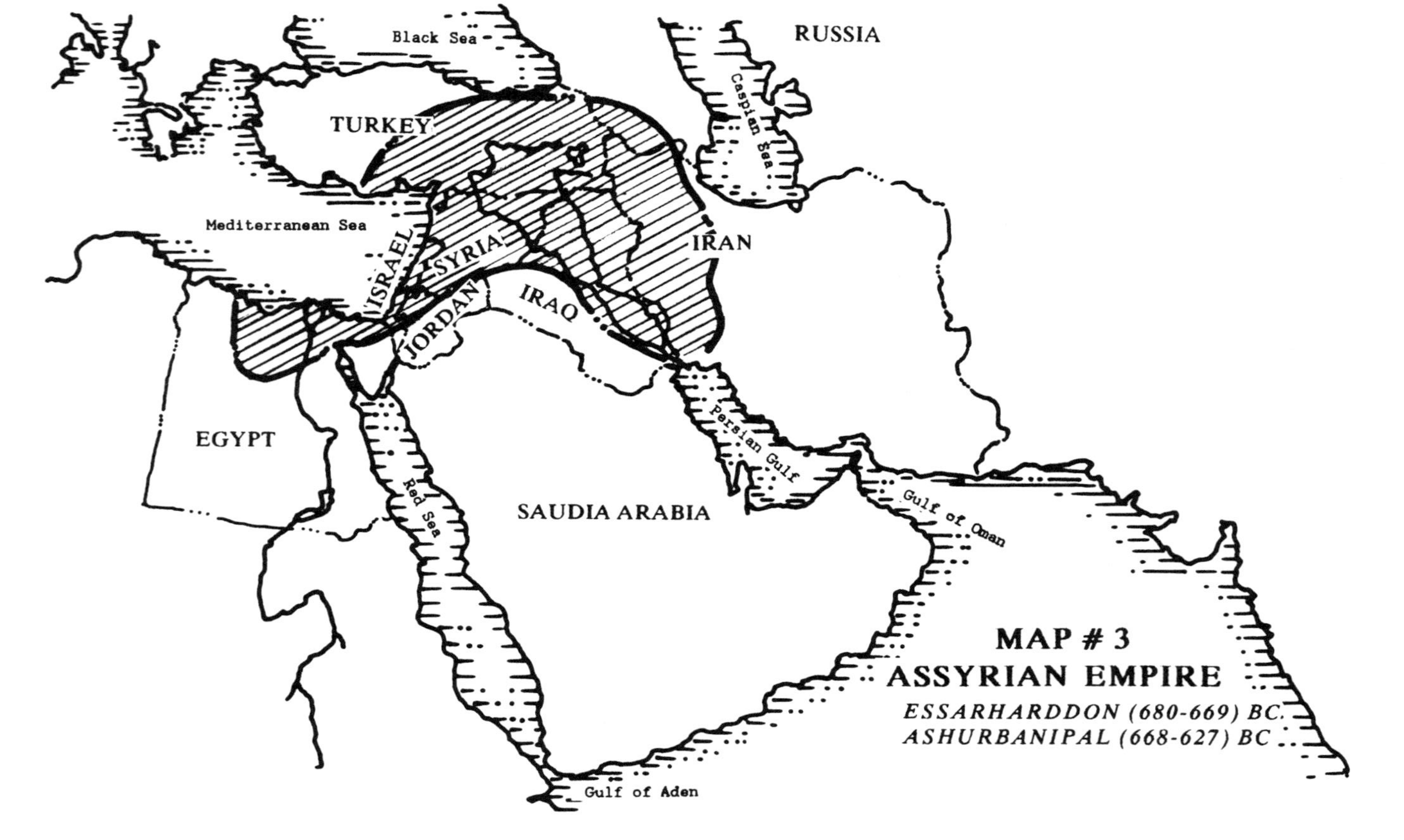
Black Sea
RUSSIA
Caspian Sea
TURKEY
Mediterranean Sea
ISRAEL
SYRIA
IRAN
JORDAN
IRAQ
EGYPT
Persian Gulf
Red Sea
SAUDIA ARABIA
Gulf of Oman
Gulf of Aden
MAP # 3
ASSYRIAN EMPIRE
ESSARHARDDON (680-669) BC.
ASHURBANIPAL (668-627) BC

10.

ARAB LEAGUE

Ezek.30:3

> *For the day is near, even the day of the LORD is near; It will be a day of clouds, a time of doom for the nations.*

There is a considerable volume of scripture dealing with the demise of the Arab nations in the Day of the Lord. Nearly all of the nations that are mentioned, can be recognized by a current map of the middle east (see map 2), and nearly all are nations that are occupied by moslem arabs. Many of the prophecies about these nations are extremely detailed, very interesting, and reflect a world tension that we are seeing unfold even as we observe.

The common bond and the PLO

Ezek.30:5

> *Ethiopia, Put, Lud, and all Arabia, Libya, and the people of the land that is in league will fall with them by the sword.*

Here is an incredible prophecy over 2500 years old that is speaking about a league of Arab nations in our own age. The common bitterness of Arab nations against Israel is the common bond which has amalgamated a conglomeration of unfriendly Moslem arabs into a unified effort to extricate Israel from the land of Palestine. The Palestine Liberation Organization (PLO) doesn't really have a place that they can call a nation, at least at the time of this writing, but this verse in Ezekiel speaks about them by referring to them as "the people of the land". There is only one land called 'the land' and that is the land of Palestine, hence I believe this verse is speaking about the PLO that is in league with these other arab nations. Beside the common bond of bitterness that unites the Arab nations against Israel, there is another bond that is perhaps even stronger, and that is their Islamic religion.

The Moslem horde

Islam is an arabic word which literally translated means something like 'submission to the will of God', and is the religion of the Moslems. Their main creed is 'there is no god but Allah, and Mohammed is his prophet'. Mohammed was the founder of Islam, which started when Mohammed made his flight (hegira) from Mecca to Medina in 622 AD. The sacred book is the Koran, much of which was derived from earlier Hebrew sources that Mohammed was acquainted with. We should be apprised of some of the unique aspects of Islam because there is scriptural evidence to support the theory that the Antichrist and/or the False Prophet will be a Moslem. The prophet (nabi) is regarded as a leader of both the spiritual and political aspects of his country, and is only superceded by an apostle (rasul). Every apostle (rasul) is a prophet (nabi), but not all prophets are apostles. Both are, however, free from grave sin, and while a prophet may fail and be killed, the mission of a (rasul) is guaranteed success by god[1], and supposedly is thus protected from human corruption.

There are five pillars of the Moslem faith:

1.) (shahada) or the confession of faith:'There is no God but Allah, and Mohammed is his prophet'.

2.) (salat) prayer 5 times a day; daybreak, noon, mid-afternoon, sunset, and evening.

---

[1] Encyclopedia of Asian History, vol.2, pg.165

3.) (zakat) almsgiving of 10% or less of the income.

4.) (festival of Ramadan) a month long fast from dawn to sunset during which the Moslems abstain from all solids and liquids. While the days are spent fasting, the evenings are spent in family feasting, socializing, and acts of piety.

5.) (haji) The pilgrimage to Mecca. "...every Muslim man or woman is duty bound to perform the rites of the Haji once in a lifetime."[2]

Another feature of Islam, which isn't considered a pillar of the faith, but which nevertheless is very important, is the concept of the (jihad) which is sometimes translated "holy war". (jihad) is fundamental to the structure of the community, and where the (dar al-islam) is threatened, it is the duty of moslems to engage in 'holy war' to protect itself. I am convinced that the arab world will enact this principle shortly, in an all out effort to finally rid itself of Israel.

It is interesting to note also, that Islam is the fastest growing religion in the Soviet Union, and that alone may account for a sympathetic relationship between the arab nations and the Soviet Union.

---

[2] Ibid. pg.168

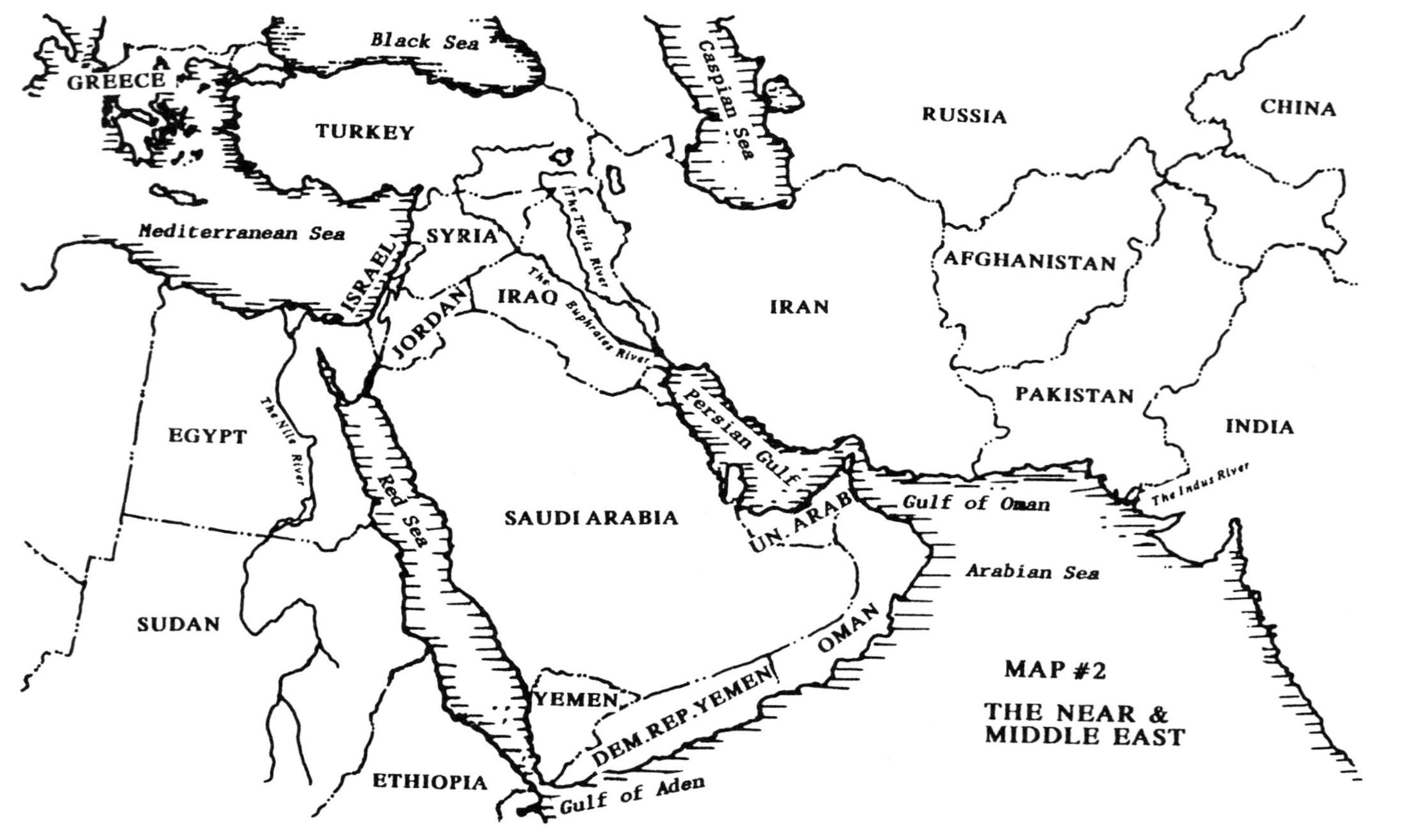
Black Sea
GREECE
TURKEY
Caspian Sea
RUSSIA
CHINA
Mediterranean Sea
SYRIA
The Tigris River
ISRAEL
JORDAN
IRAQ
The Buphrates River
IRAN
AFGHANISTAN
PAKISTAN
INDIA
EGYPT
The Nile River
Persian Gulf
Red Sea
SAUDI ARABIA
UN. ARAB
Gulf of Oman
The Indus River
Arabian Sea
SUDAN
OMAN
YEMEN
DEM.REP.YEMEN
ETHIOPIA
Gulf of Aden
MAP #2
THE NEAR &
MIDDLE EAST

Arab nations mentioned in end time prophecy

* *Ethiopia*

The nation of Ethiopia has about 43 million people and is about 40% christian and 40% moslem. It is probable that the Ethiopia spoken of in OT prophecies was a nation immediately south of Egypt, in what is now Sudan, or 'the country of the blacks' and was called 'cush'. Sudan is only about 23 million people, but 73% are Muslims. Ethiopia (cush) will be in some kind of alliance with the rest of the arab nations in the last times, and will be 'frightened' by ships from the Lord, and they will be in anguish as in the day of Egypt (Ezek.30:9). It is also listed in the armies of Gog (Ezek.38:5), and will undoubtedly be one of the nations upon which the Lord sends torrential rain, hailstones, fire and brimstone (Ezek.38:22).

* *Put*

Sometimes spelled Phut, this country was south of the country of Cush, in what is perhaps now Somalia. It is a nation of about 8 million people, 99% of which are Sunni Moslems. It is listed alongside Ethiopia in the scriptures listed above, and is adjacent to it as a nation today.

* *Lud*

In Hebrew (Ludim), and sometimes translated as Lydia (Jer.46:9), and is mentioned in conjunction with Ethiopia and Put, which leads one the conclusion it is an African nation, and perhaps Semitic since Lud is mentioned as a son of Shem (Gen.10:22).

* *Gaza (Philistia)*

This is the little area known as the 'Gaza Strip'(see map #1), and was originally known as Philistia, where the Philistines were from, and the name from which the land of Palestine apparently got its name. It has "...one of the highest population densities in the world..."[3] The occupation of the Gaza Strip by the Israeli army was begun on June 6, 1967, and the area was put under a military administration. Arab refugees, practically all muslims, swelled the population of the strip, and muslims accounted for 99% of the population. From 1967, thousands of laborers from the Gaza Strip found work in building, farming, and industry in Israel.

Both Ephraim and Judah will "...swoop down on the slopes of the Philistines on the west; together they will plunder the sons of the east." The term 'both Ephraim and Judah' refers to the combining of the two kingdoms in the end time. You will remember that Israel as the northern kingdom, was quite often at war with Judah, the southern kingdom, and Ephraim as a city in Israel, represents the entire nation. In one instance, Judah pursued Israel and 500,000 men of Israel were slain (2 Chron.13:17). After the Babylonian exile, the returning people of Judah and returning people of Israel from the Assyrian captivity were all referred to as Jews. In any case, today there is no difference between the northern kingdom and the southern kingdom, and all the tribes of Israel are clumped together without any distinction, and are all called 'Israel'. Perhaps continued terrorist activity originating from The Gaza Strip will cause the Israelis to make an air offensive upon Gaza and 'swoop down' on Gaza, and thus fulfill the prophecies of Jeremiah 47. The Lord is going to use Israel to destroy some of these Arab nations that are scheduled to be destroyed during the tribulation period, since it is also recorded that Israel will 'possess' and 'plunder' the sons of the East (Isa.-11:14).

(Jer.47:4) "...For the Lord is going to destroy the Philistines-..." (Ezek.25:15-17), The Lord will stretch out his hand against the Philistines because they acted in revenge and took vengeance to destroy with everlasting enmity. "...and they will

---

[3] Encyclopaedia Judaica, vol.7, pg.343

know that I am the LORD when I lay My vengeance on them". Over and over we see the mercy of God when a restoration and a revealing of the LORD follow judgement.

Because Gaza deported an entire population and gave them over to Edom (Amos 1:6,7,8), they will be burned to the ground, their king will be cut off, and the remnant of the Philistines will perish, and Gaza will be abandoned as a desolation (Zeph.2:4,5), and writhe in great pain (Zech.9:5).

* *Damascus*

Damascus, in present day Syria, is one of the oldest continually inhabited cities in the world, but it will meet its demise in fire and judgement because it threshed Gilead with implements of sharp iron (Amos 1:3,4);(Zech.9:1). Damascus will become helpless, will panic, and all the men of war will be silenced in that day, and she will be devoured by fire. (Jer.49:23-27). Modern Syria was once part of the Assyrian empire, and as such will most likely also be a recipient of the judgement against Assyria at the climax of the tribulation.

* *Edom*

Edom or Idumaea, Called (Mt. Seir) and (Esau) in the scriptures. These people originally were the descendants of Esau, the brother of Jacob (renamed Israel). Edom was located at the southern end of the Dead Sea, in what is now the country of Jordan. Shortly before the siege on Jerusalem in 70 AD, the Zealots sent for 20,000 Idummeans, who came to Jerusalem and committed atrocious acts of violence. "...nor did the Idumeans spare anybody; for as they are naturally a barbarous and bloody nation..."; "But the rage of the Idumeans was not satiated by these slaughters; but they now betook themselves to the city, and plundered every house, and slew every one they met;..."[4] Perhaps this action of the Idumeans is still to be punished by the Lord, or perhaps it will be because of some other malevol-

---

[4] Josephus, *Wars of the Jews,* book IV, ch.V,pg.534.

ent act. There will be 'disaster' on Esau (Jer.49:8), and "...all its cities will become perpetual ruins" (Jer.49:13). Edom will be as when God overthrew Sodom and Gomorrah, and "...no one will live there, nor will a son of man reside in it."(Jer.49:18). An earthquake accompanies the fall of Edom, and a loud noise and an outcry that is so loud that it is heard at the Red Sea (Jer.49:21). The Lord will come against Edom,"...and swoop like an eagle, and spread out His wings against Bozrah;..."(Jer.49:22). While much of the language is anthropomorphic, it certainly could apply to an Israeli air attack that wipes out Jordan. Another key verse concerning Edom is found in Ezekiel:

Ezek.25:12,13,14

> *Thus says the Lord God, "Because Edom has acted against the house of Judah by taking vengeance, and has incurred grievous guilt, and avenged themselves upon them: Therefore, thus says the Lord God, "I will also stretch out My hand against Edom and cut off man and beast from it. And I will lay it waste, from Teman even to Dedan they will fall by the sword; And I will lay My vengeance on Edom by the hand of My people Israel. Therefore, they will act in Edom according to My anger and according to My wrath; thus they will know My vengeance, declares the Lord God.*

The time indicators in this verse and chapter are 'On that day'(Ezek.24:27), which can only be the 'day of the Lord', and 'They will know my vengeance', and 'They will know that I am the Lord'(Ezek.25:14,17). This nation does not know the Lord, nor His vengeance, and has not experienced the wrath of God in this manner either, hence we conclude that the judgement is not past history, but history to be fulfilled during the tribulation period. We saw in Jeremiah where the term 'swoop' was used in conjunction with Edom's judgement, and in Ezekiel that the Lord will use Israel as His weapon, hence we believe that an Israeli air offensive will be leveled against Jordan at a near future date, and since the Antichrist dominates Israel for the last 3 1/2 years, it appears that this judgement will occur before that time. The mountains and valleys of Mt.Seir will be filled with the slain, and the nation will become a desolation and a waste (Ezek.35). One unusual prophecy about Edom is that "...I will cut off from it the one who passes through and returns."(Ezek.35:7). One possible explanation of this passage is that the land is so radioactive after the destruction, that anyone that just 'passes through' the land will die of radioactive poisoning.

Isa.34:5

For My sword is satiated in heaven, behold it shall descend for judgment upon Edom, and upon the people whom I have devoted to destruction.

These people of Edom seem to be destined to destruction by the sword of the Lord. 'For the Lord has a sacrifice in Bozrah,and a great slaughter in the land of Edom'(Isa.34:6). So awesome is their destruction, that the land will become a burning inferno, unquenched forever. Its streams will be turned into pitch and its loose earth into brimstone, and its smoke will go up forever. It shall be desolate 'from generation to generation' and 'none shall pass through it forever and ever.'(Isa.34:9,10).

Various scriptures reflect that Israel is dwelling 'securely' just before the Armageddon invasion by Antichrist and/or Gog, and since it is obvious that condition is not existing at the present time, this destruction of Edom and Gaza could well be one of the factors preceding the last 3 1/2 years that would permit a sense of 'security' in the land.

The country will be 'ransacked' and "...his hidden treasures searched out!" (Obadiah 6,7). What are the 'hidden treasures of Jordan?' One of the reasons why Edom will be destroyed, is that they 'gloated' when Jerusalem was destroyed, in the day of their misfortune, when foreigners entered the gates (Obad.11,12). Judgement will be meted out to Edom, in the same manner that they have done to others (Obad.15), and it will become as if it never existed (Obad.16), and there will be NO survivors (Obad.18).

*** Moab**

This ancient nation is within the modern nation of Jordan, which lies directly east of the Jordan river, across from the Dead Sea (see Map #1). The 'citadels' or fortresses of strength will be destroyed, the nation be consumed by 'fire' and Moab will die "...with war cries and the sound of a trumpet." (Amos 2:2). We investigated the 'war cry' and the sound of the 'trumpet' in the chapter on the translation, and have concluded that it occurs when the Lord Himself comes in wrath to judge the nations, hence we believe that Moab (Jordan) will be destroyed at the very end of the tribulation by the Lord. Historically, Moab has had an extensive relationship with Israel, and often was a refuge in times of distress in Israel. We will recall that Ruth came from Moab (Ruth 1:4), and actually entered into the bloodline of the Messiah through Joseph (Mat.1:4), so there is some kind of kinship, aside from the fact that Moab came from daughter of Abraham's nephew Lot.

*** Ammon (Jordan).**

We have already discussed the fact that Ammon was a grand-nephew of Abraham through Lot, and that Moab was his brother. Ammon was north of Moab on the east bank of the Jordan river, opposite the Dead Sea, in an area presently occupied by Jordan and Syria. Some maps show Ammon just beyond Gilead, where the tribe of Gad settled. the capital city of modern Jordan is named Amman after the ancient kingdom of Ammon, which certainly adds weight to Ammon being the nation of Jordan.

*** Lebanon**

At one time, Lebanon was a beautiful country, and Beirut was the 'pearl of the east'. The rampage and savagery of an embroiled warfare have reduced this war torn nation to piles of rubble. Internal civil strife, in a struggle for political control have created an utter chaos in this once lovely country.

Isa. 10:34

...And Lebanon will fall by the Mighty One.

The Mighty One is 'the Lord, the God of Hosts' who will 'lop off the boughs with a terrible crash (Isa.10:33), and Lebanon will be shamed and withered (Isa.33:9)

*** *Elam (southern Iran)***

In the 6th cent. B.C. Elam was a nation whose southern bounty was the north shore of the Persian Gulf, and whose northern bounty was Media. Babylon was on its west, and its capital was a city called Susa. It's present boundary would be inside Iran, just south of the Zagros Mountains. Elam is listed as one of the nations that go down to the 'nether world' (Ezek.32:18,24). It was conquered by Assyria, but some of the Elamites are mentioned in the New Testament (Acts 2:9), which demonstrates that the people were not totally eliminated. In fact, just the opposite has happened, for Jeremiah prophesied that the "...four winds from the four ends of heaven " will be brought upon Elam, and it shall be scattered to the winds. There would not be any "...nation to which the outcasts of Elam will not go." (Jer.49:34-39). The mercy of God is never ending, and at the 'last days' God promises 'That I shall restore the fortunes of Elam' (Jer.49:39).

*** *Persia (Iran)***

Cyrus the Great united both Persia and Media and succeeded in conquering Babylon in 538 BC, and Alexander the Great, a Macedonian, conquered Persia in 333 BC. The Arabs brought Islam to Persia in the 7th century, and the Turks and Mongols ruled Persia from the 11th century to 1502. The country today is 93% Shi'a Moslems. Persia is mentioned along with Ethiopia and Put (Ezek.38:5), as colleagues of Gog in his last battle against the Lord Himself. It may be worth noting that when Daniel prayed, his prayers got through, but the messenger (Angel Michael) couldn't be sent to Daniel until after 21 days because he was being resisted by '...the prince of the kingdom of Persia.'(Dan.10:13).

**** Egypt***

The number of prophecies concerning Egypt in the last times surpasses every other nation mentioned, excepting Israel.

no place to hide

Jer. 44:13

> *And I will punish those who live in the land of Egypt, as I have punished Jerusalem, with the sword, with famine, and with pestilence.*

Jews that have fled Jerusalem and gone into Egypt will be judged in Egypt, as if they had been in Jerusalem, until they are completely gone (Jer.44:27). Memphis (a city in Egypt) will be completely burned and become a desolation without inhabitants. The nation of Egypt 'will fall on an open field' and will be left there for the birds of the air to feast upon (Ezek.29:5). The land of Egypt will 'become a desolation and waste' (Ezek.-29:9). The whole land of Egypt will become an 'utter waste' even down to the border of Ethiopia.

forty year pestilence

Ezek. 29:11

> *A man's foot will not pass through it, and the foot of a beast will not pass through it, and it will not be inhabited forty years.*

The land of Egypt will become a desolation in the midst of desolate lands, and it will lay desolate for forty years. This sounds to me like a 'dirty' nuclear bomb, that creates so much radiation that the land can't be inhabited for some time. Forty years is also approximately a generation, so another reason could be that a later generation will want to return to the land of their fathers. The people of Egypt will be scattered among the rest of the nations just like Israel was, and Egypt will be reduced to the smallest among the nations. After forty years they will be gathered back into their own land again.

internal revolt

The Egyptians will be incited by the Lord 'against one another', and there will be a civil struggle or turmoil within the nation of Egypt itself. Brother against brother, city against city, kingdom against kingdom (Isa.19:2). The nation will be demoralized (Isa.19:3), and their strategy will be confounded, and they will resort to fortune telling, idols, and ghosts of the dead to try and learn what is happening.

A prophecy that may pertain to Egypt in the end times is that the leader of Egypt will have an insurrection from his own forces, and those that he thinks are his colleagues, that 'eat his choice food' will arise and 'destroy him' (Dan.11:26). It may be that this portion of scripture (Dan.11:25-28) was fulfilled in 1973 when Syria and Egypt joined forces against Israel, and did indeed 'mobilize an extremely large and mighty army' that did not stand because of schemes against it (Egypt) (Dan-.11:25). Their joint effort failed, in spite of an overwhelming advantage in equipment and men, because "...it will not succeed, for the end is still to come at the appointed time."(Dan.11:27). The huge tank army of Egypt and Syria was soundly defeated in 'The 6 Day War' by Israel. Anwar Sadat, in a surprise gesture of peace, went to Jerusalem and signed a peace agreement with Menachem Begin on March 26, 1979. The peace agreement with Israel increased tension between Egypt and Libya, which caused much civil disturbances in Egypt. On Oct.6, 1981, Anwar Sadat was assassinated by Moslem radicals from his own army.

When the civil 'war' begins in Egypt, anyone who believes in biblical prophecy would be well advised to get out of Egypt as soon as possible because the nation will be the target of nuclear weapons and total destruction will result.

geographical changes

At that time of the end, waters will dry up, and rivers will thin down to the point the fish will die and emit a terrible stench (Isa.19:5,6). The Nile is the life of Egypt and Egypt is the Nile, where the majority of the population resides within 10 miles of the river, along its 4000 mile route to the Mediterranean. At certain times of the year the water of the Nile swells and overflows its banks, providing a natural deposit of silt, and allowing agriculture to exist. When the river drys up, so will fishing, agriculture, and every industry that is dependant upon its water (Isa.19:7).

a lack of leadership

The leaders of Egypt will act like fools (Isa.19:11) and not give solid advice to their people. They are going to be lacking in wisdom, will be deceived, and even the wisest advisors of Egypt's leader will be 'stupid'(Isa.19:11). This reminds me of the advice given to Sadat by the Russians in 1972. It appears that an economic depression will be prevalent in the last days of Egypt, "And there will be no work for Egypt which its head or tail, its palm branch or bulrush, may do." (Isa.19:15). The head is the 'elder and honorable man' and the tail is 'the prophet who teaches falsehood'[5]

the fear of Egypt

Egyptians will 'become like a women', and will tremble because of the hand of the Lord of hosts that is meted out against them (Isa.19:16). Who is it that Egypt is so terrified of? It will be Israel; "And the land of Judah will become a terror to Egypt..." (Isa.19:17). Egypt should be a terrified with Israel at this very point in time, based on the past performance in every battle they have had Israel since 1948, but they don't know when to recognize defeat, and will again be defeated in battle.

change of allegiance

In that day, 5 cities of Egypt will speak Hebrew, and swear allegiance to the Lord of Hosts (Isa.19:18) and one of these cities will be named 'City of Destruction', or 'The City of the

---

5 see Isa.9:15 for similar explanation to Israel.

Sun'. The destruction of the cities of Egypt is repeated many times in different chapters and different books of prophecy, and it appears that Egypt will suffer a significant nuclear attack. Because neither man nor beast will be able to pass through the land indicates a possibility that the land will be polluted with radioactivity to such an extent that it will require forty years to dissipate. Eight specific cities are mentioned in Ezek.30 as being destroyed by Babylon. Historically, Babylon did have a war with Egypt, but Egypt was never reduced to the smallest nation of any nation, nor dispersed for forty years, nor has the land become desolate so to be uninhabitable. Neither has the land of Egypt turned to the Lord, and recognized Him; '...then they will know that I am the LORD' (Ezek.30:26). Because of these facts, I believe the prophecy has a future fulfillment in the end times. The identity of Babylon presents a bit of a problem for the end times fulfillment, since it must be the nation that the Lord uses for judgement purposes. Since both Israel and Nebuchadnezzar are mentioned, a twofold prophecy is possible with both a near and far view. The near fulfillment was fulfilled by Babylon about 606 BC, and the far view will be fulfilled by Israel at the time of the end. In a lamentation over the Pharaoh king of Egypt, Ezekiel says that they will be left on an open field, and the birds of the air and beasts of the field will feed on their flesh. The heavens will be covered and the stars darkened, and the sun will be darkened with a cloud, and there will be darkness in the land (Ezek.32:3-9).

Ezek. 32:9

> *I will also trouble the hearts of many peoples, when I bring your destruction among the nations, into lands which you have not known.*

Perhaps this is one of the things that Jesus was talking about when He told the disciples not to be frightened (Mt.24:6), and that men would faint from fear and expectation of the things to come upon the world. (Luke 21:26). This verse in

Ezekiel seems somewhat strange, but it could well be explained several ways. The destruction of Egypt that is brought among the nations and lands which they did not know could be the movement of radioactive particles in the upper atmosphere which may move the cloud into air currents that cause it to move around the globe. Nuclear fallout is going to be a major problem to everyone on earth in the event of a nuclear war. Another possible explanation is that many people of other nations will become fearful of the power of Israel when they find out what it has done to Egypt. In the first explanation, what is brought among the nations is an 'actual sample' of the destruction in the form of nuclear particles, and in the second explanation, what is brought among the nations is 'word' about the destruction.

a final solution of Egypt

Isa.19:22

And the LORD will strike Egypt, striking but healing; so they will return to the LORD, and He will respond to them and heal them.

The grace of God is so amazing! In the midst of nearly total destruction of the nation Egypt, His compassion is still extended, and His mercy still endures. Egypt will return to the Lord, and be healed by God and be exceedingly blessed.

*** Assyria (home of the Antichrist)***

Isa.10:5,6

Woe to Assyria, the rod of My anger and the staff in whose hands is My indignation, I will send it against a godless nation and commission it against the people of My fury...

Assyria does not physically exist today, and this fact is well attested to: "The collapse of the Assyrian and Babylonian civilization was so complete that its cities and remains were either wiped off the earth or buried under it, and its peoples, languages, and writings were erased from the memory of history."[6] Perhaps not totally erased though, for we do have substantial artifacts that authenticate its historicity.

Nowhere in the history of any nation have I ever read of more ruthless, bloodthirsty, rampages than that of the Assyrian Ashur-nasir-pal II (883-859 BC). Many of the annals of the atrocities are inscribed on the pavement slabs of the entrance to the temple of Ninurta at Calah, which is now represented as the Mound of Nimrod. The Assyrian Empire reached a peak of power and influence with the reign of Ashurbanipal (668-633 BC), and the following quotation quite adequately describes the nature of this man of war. "The paradox of his culture and his cruelty is well represented in the relief which shows him at a banquet in the royal pleasure garden with his queen Ashur-sharrat. The scene is one of peaceful beauty until it is noted that the head of the leader of the Elamites, whom Ashurbanipal has just conquered, hangs like ghastly fruit from the coniferous tree at the left."[7] Sennacherib (704-681 BC), conquered Hezekiah in Jerusalem, and wrote about his victories on a clay cylinder (now in the British Museum). The vivid description of the booty carried off[8] is incredibly similar to the cargoes from the allegorical Babylon (Rev.18:12,13). Even the listing of the booty starts with the same three items in the same order. I often wondered at the account in Rev. where there is a distinction made between 'slaves' and 'human lives', but in the Assyrian account this distinction is made evident, because king Hezekiah's daughters, and his concubines were sent, along with a personal messenger sent as a slave. This, of course, is just an interesting side note, because the booty captured in Jerusa-

---

[6] Encyclopaedia Judaica, vol 16, pg.1506.

[7] Finegan, *Light from the Ancient Past*, pg.216

[8] Finegan, op.cit. pg.212

lem by the Assyrians happened 700 years before John wrote the prophecy in Revelation 18. Nevertheless, the association of the historical sacking of Jerusalem by Assyria reflects the prophetic sacking of mystical 'Babylon' by a nation allegorically named 'Assyria' at the close of this age.

Another point of interest prophetically, is how many times Assyria is mentioned with respect to the 'day of the Lord', and the end times. This could be indicative of several possible answers:

1.) The prophet got his wires crossed, and made a mistake, because the nation no longer physically exists. The whole of Biblical prophecy is one of inerrant accuracy, and anyone who has examined Biblical prophecy to any depth will recognize that this reasoning is totally untenable.

2.) The nation is a figurative picture of a nation occurring in the last days that didn't physically exist during the days of the prophecy, but is characterized by the likeness of ancient Assyria. This is a possibility, especially with respect to Babylon, but is probably not the solution to the enigma because of the prophecies about even these little countries like Gaza, that have existed for thousands of years.

3.) The nation of Assyria still exists in some kind of metaphysical essence, and is embodied in a modern nation. This concept is strictly an idea, and can't be substantiated with scripture.

4.) The nation of Assyria represents a geographical area from which the present nation emerges, which will receive the judgement allocated to it. I am convinced that this is indeed a viable answer to the validity of the end time prophecies relating to Assyria (see map #3). If this concept is true, then the Antichrist, who is referred to as the Assyrian (see chapter on the antichrist), will come from the geographical area bounded by the ancient national boundaries of Assyria during its peak of power. This is an interesting theory since Assyria,

Babylon, Egypt, Meadaeo-Persia, Macedonia, and Rome all occupied the same geographical area during the peak of their kingdom age. Their boundaries were not identical, obviously, so one must outline the ancient boundaries of each kingdom during its peak of power, and see where the geographical area is that overlaps. Since we can demonstrate through scripture, that the Antichrist is from at least 4 of these nations, it seems logical that the home country of the Antichrist is located in the area subtended by their concurrent national boundaries of these ancient kingdoms at their peak of Middle East conquest. It is my contention that this is not only a plausible explanation of the nationality of the Antichrist, but correlates to a rather enigmatic portion in Revelation.

Rev. 17:9,10

> *Here is the mind which has wisdom. The seven heads are seven mountains on which the woman sits, and they are seven kings; five have fallen, one is, the other has not yet come; and when he comes, he must remain a little while.*

This is a possible explanation for the beast of 7 heads and 10 horns upon which the great harlot sits (Rev.17:3). I have thought about this passage many times without any answer, but perhaps this hypothesis is one that has some veracity. If so, it would answer one riddle, that being 'Rome', which would be the nation existing at the time of the writing of Revelation, or that which is referred to as 'one is'. But the Antichrist doesn't come from the beast that 'is' but the 'other' which 'has not come'. This beast of Rev. 17:9 is not a person, but a nation that hasn't come at the time of the writing, and yet one of the heads 'is'. I know this is very confusing, and often I wish John had labeled the beasts, beast number 1, beast number 2, etc., because the term is so general it is difficult to exactly pin down. At this moment, I think the 6 beasts before the 7th and 8th are Egypt (1400 BC), Assyria (c.650 BC under Ashurbanipal), Babylonia (600 BC under Nebuchadnezzar),

Medio-Persia (460 BC under Xerxes), Macedonia(323 BC under Alexander the Great), and Rome(120 AD), because they all have, at one time or another, occupied that specific area besides the Euphrates River, where the 7th and 8th beast will arise. It is also highly possible, according to my 'theory', that the 7th beast has come and gone already, and the 8th may be existing at this moment. Consider, that the Turkish Ottoman Empire under Solyman (1520-1566 AD), reached a zenith of occupational extent that ranged in Europe northward to Poland, Westward to the Adriatic Sea, on the east, from the Persian Gulf north to the Black Sea, and southward including all of Egypt, and it did indeed include the area of Assyria. This concept has some very interesting and significant corollaries in addition to its interesting history. Under the reign of Selim I, the empire moved through the middle east, and at Medina, Selim I took the title of CALIPH, or 'head of all Moslems' (about 1520 AD). From that time, the Caliph, or head of the empire, was also the spiritual head of all the Moslem world. The 'Janizaries', or Turkish infantry soldier, who was often a mercenary or slave, was given loot and land from the conquered provinces, which I compare to the action of the Antichrist (Dan.11:39). Solyman's navy was commanded by pirates, who succeeded in conquering the combined navy of Spain, Venice, and the pope, and brought countries on the north end of Africa bordering the Mediterranean (Algeria, Tunisia, Tripoli), into the empire. In 1801 Tripoli declared war on the United States, because the United States failed to pay tribute to Tripoli's corsair pirates. Naval campaigns forced Tripoli to concede in 1805, but it wasn't until 1815 when Algiers, Tunis, and Tripoli were defeated by a U.S. flotilla, that the piracy along the Barbary Coast was finished. In 1853 Czar Nicholas I of Russia said of the Ottoman Empire, "We have on our hands a sick man - a very sick man"[9] The saying could apply to several rulers today, which could well be successors to Solyman. By the end of the 19th century, most of the empire on the Mediterranean had fallen in the hands of Europeans. Algeria and Tunisia went to France, and Egypt to England. During World War I, Turkey fought alongside Germany and against the Allies, and in 1915, mass genocide was committed against the Armenian people which reduced a population of 1.6 million Armenian people to about 57,000.[10] Mustapha Kemal (Kemal Ataturk), an army officer, staged a revolt against the Ottoman Empire, and in 1924 a liberal democratic constitution government was formed. 1.3 million Greeks were deported; 353,000 Moslems from Macedonia were admitted to Turkey; the office of caliph was abolished; religious orders and religions were banned; and men were forbidden to wear the fez! I find it incredible that so many 'christians' today are involved in secret societies that advocate many of the 'Moslem' customs, and traditions. Such pluralistic idealism that is so diametrically opposed to biblical orthodoxy appears to me as a blatant insult to the christian ideology.

Jeremiah ch.4,10,50, refer to the kingdom that comes from the north, and is normally associated with Assyria, although in Daniel, the king of the north normally refers to Syria.

Zephaniah 2:13

> *And He will stretch out His hand against the north and destroy Assyria, And He will make Nineveh a desolation, Parched like the wilderness.*

This is a typical situation in Old Testament prophecy. The near view is that of literal Assyria being overthrown (which it was), and the far view being one that is characteristic of the

---

[9] Compton's Encyclopedia, vol.14, pg. 221.

[10] Compton's Encyclopedia, vol.1, pg.374.

last days near the end of the tribulation period. Many people will see this verse 'only' as historical past, but the context of the entire book of Zephaniah is one of wrath on the Day of the Lord, which then places (Zeph.2:13) at the end of the tribulation. The entire book of Nahum is an oracle to Nineveh, the capital city of Assyria, upon which the Lord pours out His wrath.

As we have seen in (Isa.10:5), Assyria will be used as an instrument of the Lord to bring judgement upon the subjects of His wrath, namely Jerusalem. After the judgement upon Jerusalem is completed (or nearly so), the Lord will return, and then judge the one that has been the instrument of the wrath, Assyria, and (allegorical Assyria) is in reality, a revived Moslem empire akin to the Ottoman Empire that occupied central Mesopotamia. The prophecy is one of future events at the conclusion of the tribulation period because the context of the chapter makes frequent reference to 'that day' which indicates the 'day of the Lord'. Furthermore, after the destruction by the Assyrian, Israel will truly rely on the LORD (Isa.10:20), and that certainly did not happen historically to this date.

While this chapter is intended primarily to discuss arab nations surrounding Israel, there are other nations mentioned in conjunction with them that is tantamount to the overall discussion, hence we will include them here also.

Non-Arab enemies of Israel in Ezekiel 38.

** Mesech*

Many evangelical prophetic writers, see this nation as the modern city of Moscow, but I think that may be pressing the issue well beyond the relevant information about the country. "...in the days of Tiglath-Pileser, about 1120 B.C., and Shalmaneser, 859-825 BC, the land of Muska, that is Mesech, lay in the mountains to the north of Assyria and bordered on Tabal, that is Tubal, in the west. Herodotus calls the two races the Moschoi and Tibarenoi, and locates them in the mountains southeast of the Black Sea..."[11] An examination of the Russian provinces at the northern tip of Iran, reveals Georgia, Armenia, and Azerbaidzhan,(Azerbaijan) all of which lie south of the Caucus Mountains and between the Black Sea and the Caspian Sea. Georgia and Armenia are predominately Christian, while Azerbaidzhan is Moslem. Mesech is "...a nation from Asia minor, identified today with Muski of Assyrian sources (beginning about the 12th century B.C.E.) and with (**Μοσχοι**) of classical sources."[12]

**** Magog***

Magog is the land of Gog, the end time intruder of Israel who comes to conquer and plunder the nation. Some scholars have identified Magog with Lydia[13] while others, including the historian Josephus, identifies Magog with the Scythians[14] Traditionally, Gog and his people have not been enemies of Israel, but in these end times, God puts a thought in Gog's mind, and a hook in his jaw to advance against the people of Israel. An ancient tradition also identifies Gog and Magog with the hordes that Alexander the Great locked away "..behind iron gates next to the Caspian Sea, but who are destined to break forth in the end of days."[15] Sythia "...was applied originally to the region immediately north of the Black Sea and

---

[11] Davis Dictionary of the Bible, Pg.517

[12] Encyclopaedia Judaica, vol.11, pg.1399.

[13] Unger's Bible Dictionary, pg. 684

[14] Encyclopaedia Judaica, vol.7, pg.692

[15] op.cit. pg.693

east of the Carpathian Mountains..."[16] Later on the term Scythian came to be used as we now use the word Tartars.

*** Gomer**

The nation of Gomer "...were probably Cimmerians of classical history..."[17] Kraeling shows them to be north of the Black Sea.[18] which would place them squarely in what is now USSR-

*** Togarmah**

This is a country of the far north generally identified with Armenia.[19] "The Armenians and Georgians were traditionally descended from the people of Togarmah. Later the name was applied to Turkey."[20] This nation appears in the last great battle when 'Gog' and his allies, including Togarmah, make a last all out attack on Jerusalem, and are nearly totally decimated by the hand of the Lord. (Ezek.38).

---

[16] Davis Dictionary of the Bible, pg. 729.

[17] Encyclopaedia Judaica, op.cit.

[18] Kraeling, Bible Atlas, pg.230

[19] Davis Bible Dictionary, pg.830.

[20] The New Standard Jewish Encyclopedia, pg. 1865.

11.

BIRTH OF A NATION

One of the most incredible prophecies of the Bible has to do with the birth of a nation. Not just **a** nation, but the birth of Israel. 'Aw-right now!!', you may say, Israel is already a nation! Interestingly enough, there are voluminous prophecies about the nation of Israel in the last days of this dispensation, relating it to physical birth of a baby, and specifically, the spiritual birth of Israel as a whole nation, and it is also ironic that this monumental event is mostly overshadowed by the pretrib rapture theology. This chapter is a study of the prophecies that specifically relate to the spiritual birth of Israel at the consummation of this age.

Romans 11:25,26

> *For I do not want you, brethren, to be uninformed of this mystery, lest you be wise in your own estimation, that a partial hardening has happened to Israel until the fullness of the Gentiles has come in; and thus all Israel will be saved;...*

There are many 'mysteries' within the Word of God, but this 'mystery' is about the birth of the nation of Israel after the 'fullness of the Gentiles' has happened. Paul's comment about being wise in your own estimation is peculiar, and almost sounds to me as though Paul is telling the church of Rome not to get too cocky. Why do you suppose that he would say such a thing to the body? Simply because the relationship between God and the gentile believers is somewhat of an anomaly in that the original plan of salvation through Jesus was first intended to be proclaimed by the Jews. Jesus came unto His very own people (Jn.1:11), and they rejected Him,- the very stone that the builders rejected (Ps.118:22) became the corner-stone of faith in God Almighty. The rejection of the stone by the builders is more than a clever metaphor, because it signifies something special about the term 'builder'. God's plan for Israel goes waaaay back into the dusty section of the book, where we find that God told Abraham, even while he was called Abram, that all families of the earth would be blessed through him (Gen.12:3). Even the Abrahamic covenant that God made with Abraham carried with it the 'trowel' of the builder and the 'seed' of harvest of world evangelism, by saying; "And in your descendants all the nations of the earth shall be blessed, because you obeyed My voice."(Gen.22:18). I don't know why God selected Abraham or why He decided to build a nation of Israel and unconditionally bless them, but I am sure that it wasn't because they were such a superior people physically, morally or spiritually. Ultimately, I think we shall see that Israel typifies the grace of God that unconditionally blesses, in much the same way as it does with individual christians today. Paul discusses the advantages of being a Jew, and states that they were given or entrusted with the 'oracles of God' (Rom.-3:2). It was their job to guard the words of God and be the instrument through which He could bless the rest of the world.

The Christian Jew

Rom. 2:28,29

> *For he is not a Jew who is one outwardly; neither is circumcision that which is outward in the flesh; but he is a Jew who is one inwardly, and circumcision is that which is of the heart, by the Spirit, not by the letter; and his praise is not from men,*

but from God.

The term 'Christian Jew' seems like a contradiction in terms from the Jewish point of view, since you are either Christian or Jewish, and you can't be both! There may well be room for a fourth category within the framework of Judaism, however, which could easily be labeled as 'Messianic'.

For the Christian today, there really isn't a problem, since Jesus was a Jew; all the apostles were Jews; all the writers of the New Testament, with one possible exception, were Jews; and the Old Testament was of course, done by the children of Israel. The essence and simplicity of 'Christian' often deludes query as to the intrinsic nature of 'Jew'.

What is a Jew? This question seems redundantly simplistic, but that simplicity is not as easily understood as one might first imagine. The lack of understanding this rather profound query has been and still is, the cause of many doctrinal misconceptions that have engendered deviations from christian orthodoxy which we commonly refer to as 'cults'. Appropriating promises given specifically to the physical children of Israel have caused many errors in theology, morals, and basic logic. Even the Koran is an enormous deviation of text and principles of Old Testament truths, twisted into an enigmatic dogma of confusion, deciphered only by a despotic mind bent on a system of perversion. Van Baalen has said that "cults are the unpaid bills of the church"[1] meaning that cults often fill the void created in areas that the church has neglected either doctrinally, morally, socially, or spiritually. The theology relating to the Jew is an area that even mainline churches are often unclear about, and thus becomes a target for grossly inaccurate theology to entertain. Many cults reveal their theological emphasis within the name of their organization, such as 'Seventh Day Adventism', 'Jehovah's Witnesses', and 'Moral Re-Armament'. I only mention this 'en passant' because early in

---

[1] J.K. VanBaalen, *The Chaos of Cults*, pg.390

my own experience, I was confused by very appealing literature that suggested that United States and Great Britain were, in fact, the ten lost tribes of Israel. A little study into the matter reveals errors in theology, logic, history, and archaeology, but to the neophyte, it can be very misleading. Many Evangelical Christians have erred on this point also, and insist that 'every promise in the book' is for them, because, after all, they are now the 'chosen people' of God. This is what I somewhat humorously call the 'God in the pocket syndrome', because when a person, group, or church feels that they have some exclusiveness with the Almighty, it usually reveals an error in doctrine. Just because a person has received the joy of salvation experience does not automatically make him the recipient of promises and covenants made to others in time past. Just because a person is now a member of 'The Church', which is the body of Christ, does not mean that God is going to forsake any of the other members of that very same body. Myopia is often the affliction of the 'spiritual' people of our Christian community, whose vision of the plan of God extends only to the perimeter of the ubiquitous 'I'. This shortsightedness often leads to inextricable conclusions relating to a pre-tribulation 'rapture' of the church, which totally misses one of the greatest prophetic events in the Bible. This is such a sensitive issue in the Christian community, that many Bible scholars who have arrived at the same conclusions as I, have remained silent rather than create chaos and dissention by iterating their theology.

God's desire for Israel

The apostle Paul says that 'my heart's desire and my prayer to God' for Israel, is for their 'salvation' (Rom.10:1). Paul's compassion for Israel, was very strong, and while he was a minister to the Gentiles and magnified his ministry, he hoped that somehow he 'might move to jealousy' his fellow countrymen and save some of them.(Rom 11:13,14). Paul said, 'I have great sorrow and unceasing grief in my heart' (Rom.9:2) for those unregenerate of Israel, and that, if it were even possible

'...I could wish that I myself were 'accursed'[2] for the sake of my brethren' (Rom.9:3). Paul would have given, not only his life, but his relationship with Christ, if it would bring his brethren to a right relationship with the Messiah. The compassion for Israel by Paul, in spite of the fact that he was persecuted by them, reflects the compassion of Christ for the very people He came to redeem. Jesus wanted very much to gather Israel unto Himself like a hen would gather her chicks under her wing, but Israel was unwilling (Mt.23:37). As Jesus approached the city of Jerusalem on Palm Sunday, on the week before the crucifixion, when He came as the King in the name of the Lord, 'He saw the city and wept over it' (Luke 19:41). It was the Israelites 'to whom belongs the adoption as sons and the glory and the covenants and the giving of the Law and the temple service and the promises',(Rom.9:4). Israel is the 'natural branch' of the 'olive tree' (Rom.11:17-21) which was broken off in unbelief, allowing the 'wild olive' branch (gentiles) to be grafted in. The 'natural branches' are the ones to whom **belongs** the adoption as sons, and the allowing of the gentiles to be grafted in was intended to 'make them jealous'-(Rom.11:11). The Gentile church is not an entity in itself, as most believe, but will be rejoined to the 'natural branch' when 'all Israel will be saved'. The bride will not be ready for the wedding feast until it is complete, and it will not be complete until Israel as a nation is saved. There is but one body, one bride, one church, one faith, and it is composed of both Jew and Gentile. 'God has not rejected His people...'(Rom.11:2), even though there is but a 'remnant' at the present time, that are according to God's grace (Rom.11:5). The whole of creation is anxious and suffers the pains of childbirth while longing for the revealing of the Sons of God. (Rom.8:18-23).

---

2 **αναθεμα**

The great return to the land

Throughout scripture, there has been the promise that one day Israel(the people) would return to Israel(the land) from the nations to which it was scattered. It has been the privilege of this generation to witness this prophetic phenomenon unfold before our very eyes.

Ezek.34:13

> *And I will bring them out from the peoples and gather them from the countries and bring them to their own land; and I will feed them on the mountains of Israel, by the streams, and in all the inhabited places of the land.*

Ezek.36:10

> *And I will multiply men on you, all the house of Israel, all of it; and the cities will be inhabited, and the waste places will be rebuilt. And I will multiply on you man and beast; and they will increase and be fruitful; and I will cause you to be inhabited as you were formerly and will treat you better than at the first; Thus you will know that I am the LORD.*

This modern day reversed exodus into the land has happened since 1948 when Israel became established as a nation, and the migration back to the land began. The return of the Jew to the land is one of the miracles in our age, for a people that has been without a national homeland for nearly 2000 years, has remained indigenous in the midst of repression, persecution, and mass genocide, and has still held their national identity within the nations to which they were driven.

Zech.8:7,8

> *Thus says the LORD of hosts, 'Behold, I am going to save My people from the land of the east and from the land of the west; and will bring them back, and they will live in the midst of Jerusalem,*

and they will be 'My people and I will be their God in truth and righteousness.

Quite often in scripture, there is a gap between two apparently consecutive events, and this is true of this verse. Israel will be brought back to the land, and Jerusalem will be inhabited by God's people...this has already happened, but the last part of the verse has not happened yet. Is it any wonder that the arabs are so frustrated with Israel because they can't get them out of the land? They can't get them out because it is God that has brought them back, and God is going to see to it that they are going to stay there.

The Northern Exodus

There is a distinct possibility, that the movement of Soviet Jews out of the Soviet Union at this time, constitutes what may well be called, 'the Northern Exodus'. Between 1980 and 1988, 15,752 Jews arived in Israel from the Soviet Union. During the first 3 months of 1990, over 17,000 have arrived. Soviet Jews now constitute about 6.5% of the population of Israel, which dramatically affects the philosophy and attitudes of Israel. Soviet Jews are technically skilled, educated, affluent and possess culture. Because the United States no longer sees Soviet Jews as political refugees, most of those leaving the Soviet Union will end up in Israel.

Jer.23:7,8

"Therefore behold, the days are coming, declares the LORD, when they will no longer say, 'As the LORD lives, who brought up the sons of Israel from the land of Egypt,' but, 'As the LORD lives, who brought up and led back the descendants of the household of Israel from the north land and from all the countries where I had driven them.' Then they will live on their own soil."

The tribulation temple

Most students of Bible prophecy agree that there will be

some kind of temple worship reinstalled in Jerusalem during the tribulation, and that the antichrist will step into that temple after 3 1/2 years, and commit a sacrilege (Mt.24:15; Dan.9:27). The antichrist, moreover, takes a seat in the temple and claims to be god (2 Thes.2:4). This temple has to be something special and something that I don't believe exists today. The physical spot where the old temple once was located, is now a Moslem mosque called 'The Dome of the Rock'. Whether this mosque needs to be removed and a temple built, or another temple is used is a point of conjecture, but it nevertheless is quite significant to the final chapters in the history of this age. Perhaps this is the temple that Zechariah was referring to in Zech.5, where the two angels put a woman in a bushel basket and carried her to the land of 'Shinar' where they were to build a temple for her and where she would sit on her own pedestal (Zech.5:10,11). The land of 'shinar' is the land where Babylon was built, which makes the prophecy quite difficult to understand. One possibility is that it was referring to Israel being carried away to Babylon, where it stayed captive for 70 years(606 BC). Another possibility is that it is referring to the tribulation temple, and as Israel is likened to Babylon(figuratively), so the temple is built there (figuratively). The first solution seems most logical, since the basket in which Israel was carried away in had a lead top, which could indicate that she was captive, yet protected.

How this tribulation temple comes into being, I am not sure, but somehow there **will** be a temple during the tribulation, and the antichrist **will** sit in it, **will** remove the grain offering, and **will** commit a sacrilege in it. That event will mark the half way point of the tribulation, and the time when great persecution will begin. This temple is not to be confused with a millennial temple which the Lord Himself will build (Zech.6:13). The next 2 verses speak of 'those who are far off will come and build the temple of the LORD' (Zech.6:15). If this is the same temple as Zech.6:13, then why does it say that the Lord will build it in one verse, and that those who are far off will build it in another. If it is not the same temple, is it possible that the Zech. 6:15 temple is the tribulation temple?

Israel - a force to be reckoned with

After wandering through the nations for nearly 2000 years, then being restored to their land, Israel becomes a respected force, and a nation to be dealt with. God has said that Jerusalem will be a 'cup that causes reeling to all the peoples around' (Zech.12:2). Jerusalem will be 'a heavy stone' and those who try to lift it will be severely injured (Zech.12:3). The Lord will watch over Israel, and He will make them a force to be reckoned with. God instructs them to 'arise and thresh' (Micah 4:13), and that he has made Israel to be a 'threshing sledge' among the nations (Isa.41:15,16). Jacob is identified by the Lord as 'My war club' and 'My weapon of war' (Jer.51:19-23).

Zech.12:6

> *In that day I will make the clans of Judah like a firepot among pieces of wood and a flaming torch among sheaves, so they will consume on the right hand and on the left all the surrounding peoples, while the inhabitants of Jerusalem again dwell on their own sites in Jerusalem.*

This prophecy seems quite fitting in the very day in which we live, where Israel has been regathered from the nations, established upon their own land, Jerusalem restored, and a threat among the surrounding arabs which outnumber them 10 to 1. Since becoming a nation, Israel has militarily dominated the surrounding nations like a buring fire consuming the tinder and straw. Account after account can be found of the amazing victories the Israelis have had in battle with the neighboring arabs. When the nation started, it was doubtful if its existence could be maintained with so little support and so many enemies, yet it remained, a nation born out of wedlock. In 1948 the arab nations of Egypt, Jordan, Syria, Lebanon, Iraq, and Saudi Arabia[3] invaded the land to no avail. Is it not remarkable that these same nations are also mentioned in the Bible as receiving the wrath of God in the end times? (see chapter on the Arab League).

On May 19, 1967, at the request of Egypt's President Nasser, the UN forces were removed, and the arab forces re-occupied the Gaza strip, and closed off the Gulf of Aqaba to Israeli shipping. A six day war ensued commencing on June 5th 1967, in which Israeli forces took the Gaza Strip, occupied the Sinai as far as the Suez Canal, captured the old city of Jerusalem, Syria's Golan Heights, and Jordan's West Bank. The exploits of the Israelis during the 6 day war brought tears to the eyes of prophetic Bible scholars, who knew in advance, the outcome of a war the arabs could not win, for the Lord God had already declared them victors. '...For I will restore them to their own land which I gave to their fathers.'(Jer.16:15).

On October 6 1973 (Yom Kippur), Egypt and Syria, supplied by massive Soviet airlifts, invaded Israel. Israel bolstered by an American airlift, counter attacked and drove the Syrians back on one front, and the Egyptians back on the other front, past the Suez Canal. Americans held their breath, and Bible believing Christians prayed for the peace of Jerusalem. A cease fire was initiated on October 24, 18 days after it started, with a resounding victory for Israel. The 'flaming torch among the sheaves' was victorious on the right and on the left.

A future air assault

There are a number of scriptures that indicate that Israel will defend herself with an air assault that sounds very much like 'high tech' jet fighter planes.

Isa.11:14

> *And they will 'swoop down' on the slopes of the Philistines on the west...*

---

[3] The World Almanac, pg.688

"Like flying birds
so the LORD hosts
will protect Jerusalem..."
Isa.31:5

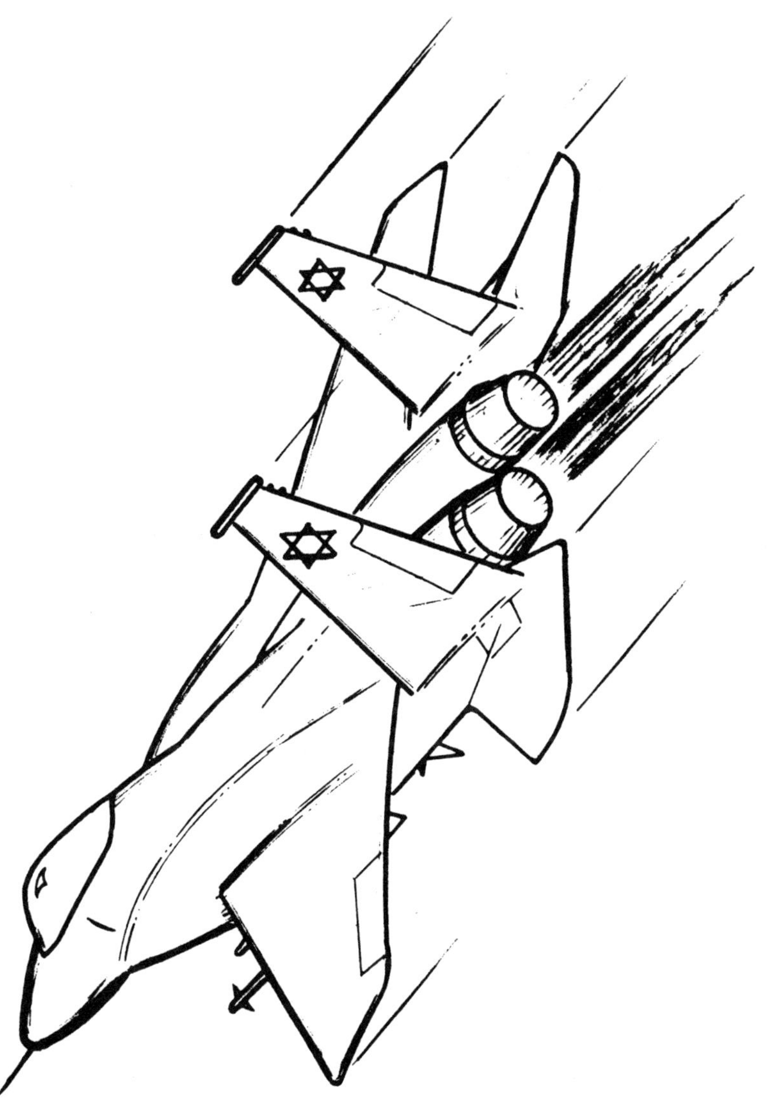

Jer.48:40

...behold, one will fly swiftly like an eagle, and spread out his wings against Moab.

It seems almost paradoxical that Israel indeed uses the F-15 Eagle in its air force.

Jer.49:22

...Behold, He will mount up and swoop like an eagle, and spread out His wings against Bozrah; and the hearts of the mighty men of Edom in that day will be like the heart of a woman in labor.

While this figurative illustration undoubtedly refers to the LORD Himself measuring out judgement against Edom, I can't help imagining a Mediterranean based aircraft carrier loaded with F-14 Tomcats with variable geometry wings.

Hos.8:1

like an eagle the enemy comes against the house of the LORD...

Hab.1:8

They fly like an eagle swooping down to devour

All does not go smooth for Israel's air offensive however, as these last two verses reveal that the enemy also has an air force, perhaps even composed of the same make and model of aircraft. The 'they' of Hab.1:8 refers to the Chaldeans whom God uses to punish Judah. Just when they are about to crush Jerusalem with the final fatal blow, the Lord comes to the rescue.

Isa. 31:5

Like flying birds so the Lord of hosts will protect Jerusalem. He will protect and deliver it; He will pass over and rescue it.

It may be that the tools that the Lord of hosts uses here to defend Jerusalem would have an eagle for a national emblem and a star in a circle with red and white stripes on the wings.

The glory fades!

Israel has been amazingly victorious in nearly every battle since her restoration in 1948, but then something is going to happen. The Lord turns the tables on Israel, and uses another nation to exercise judgement against her for 3 1/2 years.

Jer.16:9

> *For thus says the LORD of hosts, the God of Israel; "Behold, I am going to eliminate from this place, before your eyes and in your time, the voice of rejoicing and the voice of gladness, the voice of the groom and the voice of the bride.*

This certainly doesn't sound much like the ending of a 'lived happily ever after' story, and it isn't. Israel, after being extremely successful on the battlefield against arab enemies, now finds itself in a situation that it hasn't experienced in this generation. It is getting beaten, and threshed by a foreign nation. Some Bible scholars would be quick to point out that the voice of the bride is allegorically the 'Church' and the voice of the bridegroom is allegorically 'Christ'. This same illustration is used quite frequently in prophecy to describe times of sadness and mourning instead of merrymaking and rejoicing. If the meaning does reflect the Church and Christ, it would happen when the Lord physically descends upon the Mt. of Olives adjacent to Jerusalem (Zech.14:4). The kingdom of this world will then become the kingdom of the Lord (Rev.-11:15), and He will stand on Mt.Zion with the 144,000 (Rev.14:-1), who undoubtedly are the 'holy ones' of (Zech.14:5). The Lord Himself will rescue Jerusalem and all Israel just in the nick of time, before they are totally eliminated from the face of the earth. The Lord will come and fight for them, and conquer their enemies, but not before Israel has a very dark hour.

The people of Israel are going to ask the question, Why is this happening to us? What is going on here anyway? What sin did we commit that we should be judged by God in this way?

And God will answer them and explain to them the reason why:

Jer.16:11,12

> *Then you are to say to them, 'it is because your forefathers have forsaken Me' declares the LORD, and have followed other gods and served them and bowed down to them; but Me they have forsaken and have not kept My law. You too have done evil, even more than your forefathers; for behold, you are each one walking according to the stubbornness of his own evil heart, without listening to Me.*

Not only are they judged because of their forefathers, but because of the stubbornness of their own hearts. Because of the severe judgement at the hands of the Antichrist, Israel will be scattered among other nations...*again!*

Israel is going to be a force to be reckoned with for a little while longer, until the whole world becomes embroiled in bitterness against her, as a heavy stone that injures those who try to lift her. Israel will be used as the arm of the Lord to execute judgement on several of the nations round about her, such as Gaza and Edom (Jordan) and Egypt. Edom will be judged '...by the hand of My people Israel' (Ezek.25:14). Many of these other nations are specifically judged by God, but the instrument of His judgement is not specified, and could well be Israel.

Micah 4:11

> *And now many nations have been assembled against you.*

Micah 4:13

> *"Arise and thresh, daughter of Zion, for your horn I will make iron and your hoofs I will make bronze, that you may pulverize many peoples, that you may devote to the Lord their unjust gain and their wealth to the Lord of all the earth.*

But, the time will come when Israel will not be the victors, but victims.

Judgement of Israel begins

Zech.14:2

> *For I will gather all the nations against Jerusalem to battle, and the city will be captured, the houses plundered, the women ravished, and half of the city exiled, but the rest of the people will not be cut off from the city.*

Jer.7:33,34

> *And the dead bodies of this people will be food for the birds of the sky, and for the beasts of the earth; and no one will frighten them away. Then I will make to cease from the cities of Judah and from the streets of Jerusalem the voice of joy and the voice of gladness, the voice of the bridegroom and the voice of the bride; for the land will become a ruin.*

Ezek.7:3,4

> *Now the end is upon you, and I shall send My anger against you, I shall judge you according to your ways, and I shall bring all your abominations upon you. For My eye will have no pity on you, nor shall I spare you, but I shall bring your ways upon you, and your abominations will be among you; then you will know that I am the LORD!*

Every prophet from Isaiah to Malachi, with the exception of Jonah, prophesied in volumes of the judgement of Israel immediately preceding the return of the Messiah. Jonah and Nahum prophesied specifically about Nineveh, and even then we can see judgement, because 'the wicked one' (the antichrist) who comes out of Nineveh will be judged because he has become a devastator of the people of the land of Israel by 'passing through' them (Nah.1:15). The argument of the near view is often used to substantiate that the prophecies have been already fulfilled by Assyrians Tiglathpileser III(744-727BC); Shalmaneser III(854-824BC);Shalmaneser V(726-722BC);and Sennacherib (704-681); who carried off everything in Jerusalem but the kitchen sink[4] and by Nebuchadnezzar (605-594BC) the Babylonian, who plundered and carted off people, valuables, and temple treasures to Babylon. Others would cite the exploits of Vaspasian and Titus (68-70AD) when the terrible carnage of Jerusalem took place, and the temple was literally torn down stone by stone. While those mentioned came to rape, pillage and loot, they nonetheless did not fulfill the far view prophecies that speak of the 'time of distress'(Jer.14:8), 'times of trouble'(Ps.9:9)(Jer.2:27),'the time of Jacob's distress'(Jer.30:7), 'a time of distress'(Dan.12:1) which occur on the 'Day of the Lord'. We are also informed that 'immediately after the tribulation of those days'(Mt.24:29) in which those who believe are told to get out of Judea, the sign of the Son of Man will appear in the sky, and the Lord will make a physical appearance. This obviously did not happen in 70 AD when Jerusalem was destroyed, hence it is still a future prophecy, and "...Zion will be plowed as a field, and Jerusalem will become a heap of ruins... "(Micah 3:12).

We are told in several accounts that 'all' the nations will be gathered together against Israel in the 'Last Days'(Zech.12:3,9) and many nations assembled against Zion (Mic.4:11). This situation is not hard to imagine at this point in time, with Israel surrounded by hostile Arab neighbors, and oil producing arab countries placing international pressure upon Israel by using oil as political leverage. But Israel being overcome and scattered among other nations is not something we welcome hearing, yet Israel will be scattered 'as grain is shaken in a sieve'(Amos9:9).

The city of Jerusalem will suffer a tremendous blow against

---

[4] Finegan, *Light From the Ancient Past*, pg.212

it by the antichrist, and be reduced nearly to extinction. Half the city will be exiled (Zech 14:2). While the destruction will be done by the Antichrist, it is really the Lord that permits him to act as a 'hammer' against Jerusalem. He will make war against Israel and overcome it for 3 1/2 years (Rev.13:7). Antichrist will be a cruel and brutal man who will originate from 'the worst of nations' (Ezek.7:24), which will be brutal and 'ruthless' (Ezek.28:7; 30:11), and whose people are a 'fierce and impetuous people' (Hab.1:6).

Two parts of the city will be cut off and perish, and one third brought through the fire and refined like silver (Zech.13-:8). Plagues and famines will consume 1/3 of the population of Jerusalem, and 1/3 will fall by way of the 'sword' in warfare. The remaining 1/3 will be scattered to 'every wind' and pursued by the forces of Antichrist (Ezek.5:12). This sounds like total annihilation, yet there will be a few left, and some of the scattered 1/3 will be redeemed when Messiah returns. A remnant of people that will be like a few olives left in the uppermost branches after the storm has shaken off nearly all the ripe fruit.

There will be a judgement by the Lord against all those nations that attack Israel. The Lord will 'destroy completely' those nations where Israel was scattered (Jer.30:11), and will repay Babylon and the inhabitants of Chaldea for all their evil before the very eyes of Israel (Jer.51:24). Yet in spite of the severe judgement of God upon His people, and upon those who attack Israel, the Lord is waiting for repentance. If they should amend their ways and deeds, and obey the voice of God, then He will 'change His mind' about the misfortunes he has pronounced against them (Jer. 26:13).

when Israel meets Messiah

There is a phenomenon that occurs throughout the Bible with respect to Israel in the last days, wherein certain prophetic things occur by which Israel might be able to determine its relationship to the Messiah. The form of these 'indicators' are quite similar throughout the whole of the Bible. They follow a pattern of 'when' (a prescribed event takes place), 'then' (a prescribed situation will occur). An example of this is Ezek. 34:27: "...**when** I have broken the bars of their yoke and have delivered them from the hand of those who enslaved them...", "...**then** they will know that I am the LORD...". The 'when' in this passage takes place at the end of the last 3 1/2 years of the tribulation period, when Israel has been overrun and nearly decimated by the forces of the antichrist who gathers a vast army to invade and stomp out Israel, and is met by the Lord Jesus Christ (The Promised Messiah), who destroys the army of the antichrist and saves Israel from certain extinction. This scenario is repeated in different prophecies by many different prophets, at different times, from different locations. It is at this last climactic event that Israel finally realizes who Jesus is, and that He is the Messiah that they have been waiting for since the beginning. This event when "...all Israel will be saved..." (Rom.11:26), takes place at that great deliverance from the army of antichrist, and it takes place 'in a day'. In one day, the whole nation of Israel will turn to the Lord their deliverer, and receive Him as Messiah. It is this dramatic event that I call 'the birth of a nation', that the Lord has been patiently waiting for, the church has been patiently waiting for, the angels have been patiently waiting for, that Israel has been patiently waiting for, and that the devil is doing everything in his power to keep from occurring. Unfortunately the Church has become so inebriated with the concept of the 'anytime rapture' that they have overlooked the significance of this great event.

The valley of dry bones

The valley of dry bones is the theme of Ezekiel 37, and has been the theme of songs and sermons for a long time because of its unusual content. The theme is a graphic illustration of Israel in terms of a valley full of very dry bones that come to life again little by little. There is a 'rattling' of the bones, when they come together with a 'noise', and then sinews grew on them, then flesh, then skin covered them, but there was no 'breath' in them. Finally the Lord breathes on them from the four winds, and they come to life and stand on their feet, 'an exceeding great army'. This illustration is specifically revealed because God says "...these bones are the whole house of Israel-..."(Ezek. 37:11). We have witnessed this dramatic event unfold in our generation, when Israel became a nation, and people from both Judah and Israel came back to the land and established the nation in 1948. Since then, we have seen the 'sinews' come upon these bones, and the nation started to grow and flourish. We have witnessed 'the desert blossom like a rose' quite literally. In every encounter that they have had with their enemies, they have revealed a greater strength, until this very day, all that is left is the 'breath' of God, for the nation to completely fulfill the prophecy. God said "...I will place you on your own land..." (Ezek.37:14), "...and I will put My Spirit in you...". They will no longer be two nations, but they will become one nation in the land, and "...they will be My people, and I will be their God..."(Ezek.37:23). There will be an outpouring of the Spirit of God in the last days, as there was in the first days of the Church. This outpouring of the Holy Spirit on Israel will take place when Israel begins to seek after the Messiah, at the time when Jerusalem is almost ready to be obliterated by the Antichrist and the nations of the world. Jesus will return at that time and God will give Israel a heart of flesh instead of stone (Ezek.11:18).

The recognition

Zech.12:10

And I will pour out on the house of David and on the inhabitants of Jerusalem the Spirit of grace and supplication, so that they will look on Me whom they have pierced; and they will mourn for Him, as one mourns for an only son, and they will weep bitterly over Him, like the bitter weeping over a first-born.

The Lord forsook His people for a 'brief moment; but with great compassion, will regather them. He has hidden His face from Israel for a moment but with great compassion He will regather His people in the latter days (Isa.54:7,8). This recognition will occur when Israel, looking for their Messiah, sees Jesus delivering them from the persecution of the Antichrist. They will see the wound in His side (Zech.12:10), and the wounds on His hands, and they will ask Him about them.

Zech.13:6

> *And one will say to him, 'What are these wounds between your arms?' Then he will say, 'Those with which I was wounded in the house of my friends.'*

At this time Israel will **know** that the one they crucified nearly 2000 years ago was really their Messiah, and they will begin to weep bitterly and mourn like one mourns for a first born son. (Ezek.12:10-13). The blindness that has been upon Israel will be removed and they will clearly see The Lord Jesus and they will individually seek Him as Savior and Lord. The fountains will be opened for the house of David and the city of Jerusalem for sin and impurity (Zech.13:1), and Israel will experience the cleansing stream that the Gentiles have already been experiencing.

As Christians we have been taught about the Marriage Supper of the Lamb (Rev.19:9), and we have always assumed that the 'bride' that has made herself ready (Rev.19:6) was us. We have assumed that the 'wedding' (when we became Christians) was already over, and we were only waiting for the 'marriage supper' to occur. The fact is that the 'bride' won't be ready until she is without 'spot or wrinkle', that is 'complete', and that won't happen until 'all Israel is saved', and at that time the 'wedding ceremony' will take place, and the reception that we have been looking forward to will take place.

In a marriage ceremony, the minister asks the groom, 'do you take this woman to be your lawfully wedded wife?', and the groom answers 'I do'. Then the minister asks the bride, 'do you take this man to be your lawfully wedded husband?', and she answers 'I do'. This wedding ceremony is a graphic illustration of what the marriage of the Lamb is all about. The three children of Hosea are, in like manner, visual aids to illustrate to Israel the same relationship. 'Jezreel, the first son, was named (judgement), and the first daughter 'Lo-Ruhamah' (no compassion), and the second daughter 'Lo-ammi' (not my people). But after the great day at Jezreel, the Lord tells them "Say to your brothers, 'Ammi', and to your sisters 'Ruhamah'" (Hos.2:1), which means 'my people' and 'she has obtained compassion'.

Hos.2:23

> *And I will sow her for Myself in the land. I will also have compassion on her who had not obtained compassion, and I will say to those who were not My people, You are My people!"*
> *and they will say,"Thou art my God!"*

This is a beautiful illustration of a marriage ceremony when Jesus will declare His vows and the entire bride (including Israel) will declare her vows and the marriage will be finalized.

ISRAEL'S BORDERS
LEBANON
SYRIA
Golan Heights
Nazareth
Mediterranean Sea
Amman
Nablus
Tel Aviv
Jerusalem
Bethlehem
Dead Sea
Gaza
Gaza Strip
Hebron
ISRAEL
JORDAN
EGYPT
Elath
Aqaba
Sinai
SAUDI ARABIA
Gulf of Suez
Gulf of Aqaba
MAP #1
Strait of Tiran

12.

QUAKE AND SHAKE

Sounds like a Halloween 'Happy Meal' from McDonnalds, doesn't it? I was sitting in front of my TV watching the opening introductions for the World Series between the Oakland A's and the San Francisco Giants, when the picture went out. Within minutes of the temporary disruption to the baseball game, the whole nation was shocked to learn of a major earthquake that had taken place in San Francisco, even as millions of people were tuned in to the world series. I thought it to be incredible that it happened at the very moment when so many people would be watching, and at a place where so much TV coverage was concentrated for 'live' coverage. Little did they realize that they would be televising 'news' instead of 'sports', but the media was set for coverage, including the goodyear blimp that had amazing on the scene news of the quake, almost before the dust of the crumbling concrete settled. People were shocked and stunned at the awesome distruction that occurred in such a few moments of time, and were brought to realization of how fragile life really is. Bible students were particularily interested, because of the numerous prophecies relating the last days with earthquakes. We have been told for years that 'we are living in the last days' by hundreds and hundreds of Bible preachers and teachers. We also know that the Bible specifically teaches that the last times are going to be marked with violent earthquakes. How do we relate this to a timeline for the Lord's return? Are we to consider the San Francisco earthquake to be a significant sign of the last days? If it is a sign of the last days, how does the Pre-tribulation theory line up? For that matter, how does ANY tribulation theory line up to the front page of the newspapers about earthquakes? Is there a connection between the location of the earthquake and the activity of gross immorality in the SF Bay area? Should we say, as Fred Sanford, "This is this the big one Elizabeth!"?

The Beginning of the End

MT.24:7,8

> *For nation will rise against nation, and kingdom against kingdom, and in various places there will be famines and earthquakes. But all these things are merely the beginning of birthpangs.*

For years we have been taught that the different wars that we have had were indicators of the coming time of tribulation, since natiion did rise against nation and kingdom did rise against kingdom..didn't it? Would you believe that the word for 'nation' in the greek text is the same root word that we get the word 'ethnic' from? Matthew 24 is one of the most maligned passages of scripture in the entire Bible. Seemingly, everyone who reads the chapter becomes a compulsive prophet who completely understands all he reads, and and has a scheme by which he is able to put these things into 'proper perspective' with respect to some type of timeline graph that shows when the 'rapure' will take place. The overwhelming majority of Evangelical Christians accept Matthew 24 to reflect happenings during the last seven year 'tribulation' period, which takes place after the 'dispensation' of the church age comes to a close. Maybe so, maybe no. If the translation occured prior to the tribulation, then the church would not see ANY signs at all, because the signs are inclusive of the tribulation events.

Birthpangs is an extremely interesting term, and is found frequently in the OT prophecies relating to the end times. It is a study all to its own, and diserves a complete chapter to trace though the scripture and determine a precise meaning. We are, however, going to leave that task for another occasion. If earthquakes are the beginning of birthpangs, and birthpangs are a the beginning of the tribulation, are we then to infer that we are NOW into the tribulation? If that was all that we had to determine the tribulation by, then it would be a definite maybe. We do have many other indicators which must, like little ducks, all be in a row. If earthquakes are a signal of the beginning of birthpangs, then it would seem what we are now experiencing would be considered 'false labor'. That is, before the actual labor for childbirth begins, a woman often experiences Braxton-Hicks contractions, which are not the real thing, but are very similar. They are another indication that the REAL birth pains are coming soon, and I feel that is what the earth is experiencing at this very time. We must also realize that as far as earthquakes go, this recent quake in San Francisco hardly ranks with the rest of the 'major' quakes in time past. Within our lifespan, for example, there was the 87 quake in Ecuador that claimed over 4000 lives and was rated as 7.3 Richter, and the 85 quake in Mexico City that claimed over 4200 lives and was rated 8.1 Richter. As terrible as these quakes were, they pale in comparison to the quake of 1976 in China that cost 242,000 lives, or Calcutta, India 1737 that claimed 300,000 lives. The worst quake I can find recorded was 1556 in China, that cost 830,000 lives. The degree of intensity of end time quakes will be a factor, but I am convinced that the frequency may be an even more significant factor. This idea seems regnant in the statement 'various places', which I deem to mean various places at the same time. Some places, like San Francisco, have a history of quakes, and the people that live there have come to accept it as a constant threat. 'Various places' seems to indicate that there will be quakes in areas that don't normally experience them. This is going to be the time when the earth 'totters', and wobbles 'to and fro', perhaps (if I can speculate), even alter its normal rotation, or shift on its axis. In conjunction with the earth quaking and shaking, there will be astronomical changes that will cause the Moon to take on a 'red' appearance, and the Sun to become darkened. Seasons of the year are going to become confused, and there will be winter when it isn't supposed to be winter, and a condition will occur that will be neither daylight nor night. I'm sure many people will think this sounds 'Science-Fiction-ish', but thats what the book says is going to happen.

Quakes and Prophets

There are some things relating to earthquakes and prophecies that I think are interesting and worth repeating.

Zech. 14:5

> *And you will flee by the valley of My mountains, for the valley of the mountains will reach to Azel; yes, you will flee just as you fled before the earthquake in the days of Uzziah king of Judah. Then the LORD, O My God, will come, and all the holy ones with Him.*

* The earthquake mentioned by Zechariah as having taken place in the days of Uzziah is mentioned again by Amos (Amos 1:1), and is apparently confirmed by Josephus. The earthquake in the last days will be similar to the one during the days of Uzziah, because the people will flee before it in the same way.

* You may recognize the passage from Zech. as being from the section that tells about the Lord returning to the mount of Olives, and having the mountain split under His feet from east to west, creating a great valley through which the Jewish Remnant will flee.

* This may well be the very same event as spoken of by John in Revelation 16:19 when the 7th bowl judgement is poured out upon the earth, "And the great city was split into three parts, and the cities of the nations fell..." If you are a student of the Bible you may recognize the mystery and controversy within that verse.

* Some students are 'sure' that this verse reflects a pre-trib viewpoint, because it says that the Lord is returning with His 'holy ones with Him', and that surely must mean that the Christians coming **with** Him, will have already been 'raptured' at some prior time. The problem with that logic is often overlooked by presupposing that the 'holy ones' refers to resurrected Christians. We are not specifically told that Christians will be with Him when He returns, but we are specifically told that angels will accompany Him.

Mt 25:31

But when the Son of Man comes in His glory, and all the angels with Him, then He will sit on His glorious throne.

Mt.16:27

For the Son of Man is going to come in the glory of His Father with His angels; and will then recompense every man according to his deeds.

Also see Mk 8:38; Mk.13:27; Lk. 9:26 - which also refer to Jesus returning with His angels. Furthermore, Job 5:1; and Ps.89:5,7 quite conclusively point to 'angels' as being referred to as the 'holy ones'. We know that the Lord will bring angels with Him when He returns, but to categorically state that He will also bring all believers which have been with Him for 7 years prior to that, is a highly speculative and tenuous position that cannot be clearly demonstrated from the Scriptures.

Tribulation quakes

With the breaking of the sixth seal, a significant uniqueness occurs. The people of the earth from every strata, whether upper eshelon or peons hide in caves and among the rocks of the mountains, trying to get away from the presence of the Lamb.

Rev. 6:12

And I looked when He broke the sixth seal, and

> *there was a great earthquake; and the sun became black as sackcloth made of hair, and the whole moon became like blood;*

Again, with the breaking of the seventh seal, an earthquake occurs:

1. peals of thunder
2. sounds
3. flashes of lightning
4. earthquake

Rev. 8:5

> *And the angel took the censor; and he filled it with the fire of the altar and threw it to the earth; And there followed peals of thunder and sounds and flashes of lightening and an earthquake.*

Similarities between events of the different jugements have caused some to conclude that they are, in fact, the same event, and that the timing of the series of judgements to be concurrent. Similarities, however, do not necessarily become an identity, and I am not convinced these earthqukes are the same. The intensity of these quakes continues until we reach the seventh bowl judgement, that brings everything to a catyclismic climax, and marks the end of the great tribulation. The voice that comes from out of the temple says 'It is Done'.

Rev. 16:18,19

> *And there were flashes of lightening and sounds and peals of thunder; and there was a great earthquake, such as there had not been since man came to be upon the earth, so great an earthquake was it, and so mighty. And the great city was split into three parts, and the cities of the nations fell...*

Quake and Shake

The Shakers

Mt. 24:6

And you will be hearing of wars and rumors of wars; see that you are not frightened, for those things must take place, but that is not yet the end.

Jesus is specifically instructing His disciples, not to be frightened...which pre supposes that the disciples would have something to be frightened about. If that were not so, the exhortation would be meaningless. Assuming that 'we' or othera believers will be present when the tribulation does occur, it almost seems like the Lord is asking quite a bit of us by telling us not to be frightened. Luke uses a little different word, Lk.21:9 (terrified), in a parallel passage, that perhaps includes the concept of 'terror'.

James 5:7,8

Be patient, therefore, brethren, until the coming of the Lord...You too be patitent; strengthen your hearts, for the coming of the Lord is at hand.

The Lord frequently gave His disciples, and us, encouragement and exhortation to tranquillity, as illustrated by these scriptures:

Jn. 14:1

Let not your heart be troubled; believe in God, believe also in Me.

Jn. 14:27

Peace I leave with you, My peace I give you; not as the world gives, do I give to you. Let not your heart be troubled, nor let it be fearful.

Luke 21:26

Men fainting from fear and the expectation of the things which are coming upon the world; for the powers of the heavens will be shaken.

The Last Trump

OK! - So the Bible says there are going to be earthquakes all through the tribulation from the very beginning to the vbery end, and we are not supposed to get the 'shakes' in the 'quakes', that is we are not to be frightened, because the Lord has everything under control, and He will not permit us to be judged in the same manner as the world is judged. Whether beievers are raptured prior to the tribulation, or at a time near the very end (as I believe), we need to establish when the tribulation officially begins, to be able to identify whether some of these signs are to be considered viable or not.

The Beginning of the End

I am convinced that the actual beginning of the tribulation period of seven years, will be initiated by an activity of the Antichrist, who signs a seven year peace pact:

Dan 9:27

> *And he will make a firm covenant with the many for one week, but in the middle of the week he will put a stop to sacrifice and grain offering;...*

It is not very fair to pull part of one verse out of this rather enigmatic section, and I trust you will study it yourself. The 'he' in Dan. 9:27 is the Antichrist, who makes a 'firm covenant' which is some type of peace pact, perhaps simialar to the one between Begin(Israel) and Sadat(Egypt) on March 26, 1979. This covenant will be between Antichrist and his forces (which may not even be a nation at the time), and Israel, which will allow the Jews to begin temple worship, and provide, what I call, a 'land for bux' deal. If I am correct, he may even be a candidate for the Nobel Peace Prize for his ingeneous (allbeit temporary) solution for the Palestinians in the Middle East. I understand the 'one week' of the covenant to mean a seven year period of time. I believe it can be demonstrated that the 'middle of the week' means 3 and 1/2 years. That is, after 3 1/2 years, the antichrist steps in and stops the sacrifice in the temple, and desecrates the sanctuary in what is known as 'the abomination of desolation' and which is refered to in such passages as Dan 9:27; Dan 11:31; Dan 12:11; Mat.24:-15; Mark 13:14; 2 Thes 2:4. The very fact that there is a 'sacrifice' and a 'grain offering' indicates that the temple worship will have been reinstituted. For this to happen, several other things must also take place that sets the stage for tribulation circumstances to transpire. It is my understanding that before the temple worship can be officially restored, the 'kalal' must be found with the ashes of a red heifer that is necessary for a ceremonial clensing before the sacrifice can be authentic. This may sound rather strange if you have not studied the Old Testament closely, but if you start at Numbers 19, you can see where this concept came from originally.

Some have said that the first half of the tribulation period (3 1/2 years) will be a time of propsperity. I see war, famines, earthquakes, racial tensions, a comet hitting the earth, tidal waves, undrinkable water, an indundation of insects, and if that is not enough, - a Satanic individual that runs around like a mad man, lopping heads off believers. I don't see much prosperity there at all. What short lived peace that is ironically hailed as triumph, will reflect that which Jeremiah said a thousand years ago:

Jer. 6:14

> *And they have healed the wound of My people slightly, saying, 'peace, peace', but there is no peace.*

The Last Trump

13.
A LOOSE CANNON

A 'loose cannon' is a term which I think, was probably coined by the pentagon to describe an individual, group or entity, that possesses considerable power either politically or militarily, and that cannot be relied upon to act in a manner originally intended when the power was delegated. The illustration of a loaded cannon with its fuse lit, swinging around out of control, and pointing back at the one that lit the fuse is quite appropriate. It is my contention that the Antichrist will ultimately be considered a 'loose cannon', because no one will be able to determine what he will do next, or what means he might use. Terrorism is a term that this generation has become accustomed to hearing, but not accustomed to being intimidated by. The Antichrist will be a master of terrorism, and will deploy it to his own interests. It is interesting to note the number of scriptures that seem to indicate the use of terrorism by countries that are allies to the antichrist forces in the last days.

The following is a list of terrorism that has originated from Arab forces that was gathered from various sources.

Nov.4 1979, seizure of US embassy in Teheran lasting 444 days.
Ap.18.1983 - car bombing of US Embassy in Beirut, 63 killed.
Oct.23,1983 - suicide bombing of US Marine & French barracks in Beirut. 241 Americans killed, 58 French killed.

Nov.4,1983 - car bomb - Israeli post in Lebanon. 60 die.
Dec.12, 1983 - car bomb attacks against US in Kuwait, 7 killed.
Jan 18, 1984 murder of Malcolm Kerr, president of American University of Beirut.
Feb.7, 1984 - assassination of former Iranian Gen Gholam Oveisi, Paris.
Mar.7, 1984 - kidnapping of CNN reporter Jeremy Levin
Mar.16, 1984 - kidnapping of CIA Beirut station chief William Buckley, died in captivity.
May 8, 1984 - kidnapping of Rev. Benjamin Weir.
Sept.20, 1984 - truck bombing of US Embassy annex, Beirut; 14 killed.
Dec.3, 1984 - hijacking of Kuwait airflight 221 to Teheran
Jan.8,1985 - kidnapping of father Lawrence Martin Jenco.
Mar.16,1985 - kidnapping of AP reporter Terry Anderson.
June 9, 1985 - kidnapping of Thomas Southerland, dean of American University of Beirut.
June 14, 1985 - hijacking of TWA flight 847, US diver murdered.
Jul.22, 1985 - bombing of NW Orient office, and a Synagogue in Copenhagen.
Oct.7, 1985 - Italian cruise ship 'Achille Lauro' hijacked by PLO. Leon Klinghoffer killed.
Nov.23, 1985 - arab gunmen seized Egyptian jetliner from Athens to Cairo. 60 people killed.
Dec.7, 1985 - bombing of 2 department stores in Paris.
Dec.27, 1985 - Palestinian terrorists kill 20 civilians in airports in Rome and Vienna.
Sept.9, 1986 - kidnapping of American Frank Reed in Beirut.
Sept.12, 1986 - kidnapping of Joseph Coppio in Beirut
Sept. 1986 - series of Bombings in Paris, 9 killed. 20 killed by 2 terrorists in a synagogue in Istanbul.
Oct. 21, 1986 - kidnapping of American Edward Tracy.
Jan.20, 1987 - kidnapping of Beirut University college professors Jesse Turner, Alan Steen, Robert Polhill and Mithileshuar Singh.

May 16, 1987 - Iraqi missiles kill 37 in attack on US frigate 'Stark'.

June.17, 1987 - kidnapping of ABC journalist Charles Glass in Lebanon.

July 24, 1987 - hijacking of Air Afrique jet.

Oct.13, 1987 - Iranian missile hits near school in Baghdad, killing 32, nearly all pupils.

Nov.26, 1987 - Arab guerrillas kill six Israeli soldiers. palestinians fly motorized hang gliders in raid on base.

Feb. 17, 1988 - kidnapping of marine Lt. Col. Richard Higgins, a UN observer in south Lebanon.

March 7, 1988 -6 die as Palestinians hijack Israeli bus.

April 5, 1988 - hijacking of Kuwaiti Airlines flight 422, two murdered.

April 14, 1988 - 5 killed by bomb in Naples USO club.

Spring 1988 - worldwide terror campaign against Saudi Arabia.

June 12 ,1988 - Palestinian arsonists are blamed for the destruction of Israel forrest.

July 11, 1988 - terrorists kill 9 on Aegean cruise.

Dec. 21, 1988 - Pan Am flight 103 was exploded over Scotland killing all 200 plus civilian passengers. The bomb was determined to have been a plastic bomb hidden in a radio-cassette player ostensibly placed there by a member of the Achmed Gemile group of the PLO.

American policy on Terrorism

As a result of the threats of terrorists, the U.S. has formulated a three fold policy in its official stand against terrorism.[1]

---

[1] Paul Bremner III, *Countering Terrorism in the 1980's and 1990's,* Dept. of State Bulletin, Feb.1989, pg.61.

1.) America will not accede to terrorists demands, and will not pay ransom or pardon convicted terrorists, or pressure other countries to give in to terrorists demands.

2.) America as taken the lead in pressuring states which support terrorist groups and which use terrorism as a part of their foreign policy. This second point should be stated so strong as to bear its teeth. Actions by nations such as West Germany, that has provided the technology to build the worlds largest chemical warfare plant in Libya, should not be tolerated. Nations that provide nuclear weapons to Pakistan and other third world countries should be made responsible. It is no more reasonable for any nation to supply weapons of destruction to countries that have a proven track record of terrorism and aggression, than it is to supply a convicted killer with an automatic weapon. It just doesn't make sense!

3.) America is imposing a 'long arm statute' on terrorists, which makes it a Federal crime to kill, injure, threaten, detain, or seize an American citizen anywhere in the world in order to compel a third person or government to accede to a terrorist demand. The upshot of this statute is that an identified terrorist that has committed a crime of terrorism against the United States, will be pursued and arrested anywhere in the world, by the 'long arm' of the law.

Terrorist groups of immediate concern

There are three different sources of terrorism that are an immediate concern to the United States at present, and they are:

1.) Palestinian Groups such as those led by Abu Abbas, Abu Nidal, Achmed Gebriel, and Abu Jihad (Khalil al Wazir).

2.) Libya - who has openly sponsored terrorism against the U.S.

3.) Latin American Terrorists - financed by 'big money' narcotics dealers who hire them to protect their illicit drug trans actions.

Where is terrorism leading?

I have listed the specific acts of terrorism because I am convinced that the Antichrist is going to use these tactics to escalate his power and authority. Jesus said specifically that because lawlessness is increased most peoples love will grow cold, (Mt.24:12), and Antichrist is called 'The Lawless one' (2 Thes.2:8). He is called 'The man of lawlessness', (2 Thes.2:3), and associated with the 'Mystery of Lawlessness' (2 Thes 2:7). His followers not only believe his lies, but take pleasure in wickedness. People become so callous and perverted that they become drunken with the sensuousness of sin. Jude alludes to this, saying that the wicked will be 'following their own ungodly lusts', (Jude 18). Peter tells of the type of people who will be existing in the last days - 'mockers following their own lusts', (2 Pet.3:3).

Hedonism seems to be prominent in our society today, where people follow after anything and everything that provides satisfaction for their desires. People will become like robots, blindly following after sensuality (2 Pet.2:2). Even the teachers they have will be teaching them things that satisfy their own ears. They will be 'lovers of self' and lovers of 'pleasure rather than lovers of God' (2 Tim 3:4). I suppose that preachers have been saying that these scriptures applied to their generation since the beginning of the Church, and most people reading this will probably think that these scriptures are so general that they really aren't significant to our generation any more than any other. I see 'catch phrases' that indicate that this applies to our generation as well. 'I love me' is a phrase that I see appearing frequently, and the concept of 'me first' and 'look out for number one' characterize much of our self centered society today. The really sad part of all this is that people really won't know any better, because their very conscience's are cauterized and calloused to the point of being totally insensitive. (1 Tim.4:2).

Fear and terror go together

Jesus specifically said "...there will be **terrors** and great signs from heaven' (Luke 21:11). Believers are told by the Lord not to be frightened, (Mk.13:7), or as Luke records it, 'do not be **terrified** (Lk.21:9) at the wars and disturbances that will take place during those few years. Antichrist will be a master at developing 'fear' in people, but Jesus casts out fear and replaces it with love. There is no fear in love but 'perfect love casts out fear' (1 Jn.4:18). As a matter of fact, God doesn't want us to be 'wimps', He wants us to act mature and without fear (2Tim 1:7). Fear is one of the tactics that Satan uses to keep people in bondage as slaves to sin, but God has freed us from that power (Rom.8:15).

God judges terrorism

Isa.17:14

> *At evening time, behold there is terror! Before morning they are no more. Such will be the portion of those who plunder us, and the lot of those who pillage us.*

This appears to be the judgement of God upon those nations that have been oppressors of Israel in the last days. They will meet their untimely demise at the hand of the Lord, who may use the weaponry of a technologically advanced nation as His instrument of judgement.

Isa.19:17

> *And the land of Judah will become a terror to Egypt; everyone to whom it is mentioned will be in dread of it, because of the purpose of the Lord of hosts which He is purposing against them.*

Here the object of terror is reversed. Instead of Antichrist being the terror of the world, Israel becomes a 'terror' to her enemies. Their fear is quite justified, because every one of Israel's neighbors will be reduced to rubble (see map #1).

Isa. 24:17,18

> *Terror and pit and snare confront you, O inhabitant of the earth. Then it will be that he who flees the report of disaster will fall into the pit, and he who climbs out of the pit will be caught in the snare; For the windows above are opened, and the foundations of the earth shake.*

The fear of the Chaldeans will precede them, and they will plunder and destroy other nations. They won't follow any guidelines for warfare either. Neither the Geneva rules nor United Nations will mean anything to them because they will make their own rules.

Hab. 1:6,7

> *For behold, I am raising up the Chaldeans, that fierce and impetuous people who march throughout the earth to seize dwelling places which are not theirs. They are dreaded and feared. Their justice and authority originate with themselves.*

This concept of being their own judge and jury or making their own laws as they go is characteristic of the Antichrist (Dan.7:25) who will intend to make alterations in the law. His law is really 'no law at all' and for that reason Paul calls him 'the man of lawlessness'[2] (2 Thes. 2:3).

It is more than coincidental that Ezekiel is given a word from the Lord to wail for the multitude of nations that have been designated to the 'nether world', as being the same nations that come against Israel in the last days, and that are the kingdom of the Antichrist. These nations are Egypt, Assyria, Elam, Meshech-Tubal, Edom, and Sidon.

---

[2] **α—νομοσ** literally, 'without law'

Assyria spread 'terror' in the land of the living (Ezek.32:23). Elam instilled their 'terror' in the land of the living, and bore the disgrace of those who went down to the pit (Ezek.32:24,25), and the same thing is said of Mesech-Tubal (Ezek.32:26). The 'princes of the north' and Egypt are there also.

Is it not strange that the very people who are today know as 'terrorists' who perpetrate aggression against Israel, come from these same countries?

14.

GOOD GRIEF! WHAT NEXT?

The Pepsi Generation

One of the questions that I am most frequently asked is, 'What is going to happen to America?' I guess it is natural for people to be concerned with what is going to happen to them in the future, but most often, it is because we are concerned that God's plan may interfere somehow with our comfort zone. We are the 'Pepsi Generation'!!! We are the generation that demands instant attention, whether it's an automatic vending machine or a fast food restaurant. We will leave 10 minutes late for work, then drive 80 miles per hour to get there on time, and get upset because someone is actually driving the speed limit ahead of us, which will cause us to be late. We put the change in the machine, pull the knob, and we want action, right now! It is incredible how much our society has learned to take for granted the things that our parents would have considered luxury items, (if they were even available). Truly, our generation is extremely self centered, egotistical, and hedonistic. Somehow I think our attitude toward the world around us reflects the relationship that we have with God as well. We will spend a few minutes every once in a while in prayer, if it doesn't interfere with our schedule of events for the day. We may spend some time reading the Word of God, providing we won't miss any of that special TV soap opera that is so risque that the little ones have to leave the room so we can watch it. One of the tenants of our faith is

The Last Trump

Yet those who wait for the Lord
Will gain new strength;
They will mount up with wings like eagles,
They will run and not get tired,
They will walk and not become weary.
Isa. 40:31

'Wait', but that is not in our vocabulary today. When we pray, we expect God to answer and respond like some kind of celestial bell hop that pops out and attends to our beckoning call whenever and wherever we happen to call on Him. Not only is He supposed to respond instantly, like making a cup of instant coffee, or getting a candy bar out of the vending machine, but we don't even ask anymore, we tell Him. After all, we are the King's kids, right? Since He is the King, and we are His kids, we should have everything that royalty is supposed to have, right? I am of course making light of our relationship with God, but I really wonder if God doesn't consider us 'spoiled brats' sometimes. I think we have all seen this type of child at one time or another. Their parents are wealthy, and they demand of them whatever they think they want at the time, and make such a scene with whining and carrying on that the parent capitulates and provides whatever the kid wants. I wonder if God thinks of us a constant 'whiners', like some impetuous child that demands his parents cater to his every whim and fancy?

Ezek. 14:13,14

> *Son of man, if a country sins against Me by committing unfaithfulness, and I stretch out My hand against it, destroy its supply of bread, send famine against it, and cut off from it both man and beast,*
>
> *even though these three men, Noah, Daniel, and Job were in its midst, by their own righteousness, they could only deliver themselves, declares the Lord God.*

Is America free from the judgement of God just because there are some Christians that live there? Are we to assume that God is going to spare our nation because we are so important that we will stay the hand of God in judgement? I think the text here is pretty clear, that should God judge America, the only ones that will come through will be the righteous people who are declared righteous by God. Incidently this chapter in Ezekiel doesn't stop with famine, it continues with wild beasts, a sword, a plague, and ultimately, the wrath of God poured out upon a people that deserves judgement.

Nuclear war

When I was a young boy growing up in the 50's there was a constant threat of nuclear war, and everyone speculated about world war III. Would we become involved in an all out nuclear war with Russia? Would we have a terrible ground war with China? Thirty five years later there is still the threat of war with Russia, except now the weapons have become so large and sophisticated, the very thought of war is not unlike a science fiction novel. Intellectuals who speculate on a nuclear war, such as Carl Sagan, think in terms of a nuclear winter (assuming that there are any survivors at all). Thermo nuclear fusion weapons of 100 megaton range are about 1000 times more powerful than the fission weapons used on Japan during World War II. We have counted heavily on a philosophy that a good offense is the major deterrent to nuclear aggression. Nobody in their right mind would dare to begin a war that nobody could win, and everybody would loose. Until now, that philosophy has worked fairly well, not with standing the 'cold' war in Korea, and Vietnam. As terrible as these wars were, they can not be compared to an all out nuclear war. The threat of nuclear war was pretty much held in check until now, because the nations that possessed nuclear weapons was held to a handful of mutually exclusive nations that possessed high technology and had respect for one another. All that has now changed! Third world nations such as India, who acquired 'the bomb' cannot be counted upon to respect a 'gentleman's agreement'! Unilateral non proliferation agreements and detente means absolutely nothing to third world countries with a 7th century mentality, who are totally committed to destroy anyone who disagrees with their leaders. Oil rich arab nations will succeed in 'buying' nuclear devices and attempt an offensive to destroy Israel. Nearly everyone concedes that Israel is a nuclear power, even though they have never officially exploded nuclear devices. This also is going to change in the near future!!

Israel is going to deploy short range nuclear devices to annihilate the Arab nations that surround them. Observe map #1 for a moment, and note the borders of Israel today. Every one of these neighbors are going to be destroyed by nuclear weapons! So what makes me think that the Bible tells about a nuclear war in the end time?

Clouds and darkness

It is a well known fact that nuclear explosions produce upper atmospheric disturbances and strange clouds. "...that I shall make the sun go down at noon and the earth dark in broad daylight." (Amos 8:9). The day of the Lord is called a 'day of clouds' and 'a time of doom for the nations' (Ezek. 30:3). In a city in Egypt called Tahpanhes, the 'day will be dark' and a 'cloud will cover her' (Ezek. 30:18). Ezekiel again prophesies concerning Egypt saying that the 'stars' will be darkened; the sun covered with a 'cloud'; the moon will not give its light; all the heavenly lights will be darkened; and a darkness will be over the land. (Ezek. 32:7,8). The people who are considered 'Gods sheep' will be delivered on 'a cloudy and gloomy day' (Ezek. 34:12). The day of the Lord, will be a 'day of darkness and gloom; and a day of 'clouds and thick darkness' (Joel 2:2). There will be wonders in the sky, and on the earth, 'blood, fire and **columns of smoke**' (Joel 2:30).

Red moon and dark sun

Joel 2:31

> *The sun will be turned into darkness, and the moon into blood, before the great and awesome day of the LORD comes.*

At one time, I thought this phrase was a metaphorical expression intended to convey despair and depression, but I think it may be a physical condition caused by dust particles in the upper atmosphere that makes the moon appear blood red in color, and the sun to be significantly darkened. It is this same setting that Jesus is referring to when He says;

Mat. 24:29

> *But immediately after the tribulation of those days, the sun will be darkened, and the moon will not give its light, and the stars will fall from the sky, and the powers of the heavens will be shaken.*

Something quite unusual is going to take place with the sun and the moon, so much so that it will be considered as a 'sign' (Luke 21:25). Perhaps it is on the backdrop of nuclear clouds that Jesus will appear, coming 'on the clouds of the sky' (Mat.24:30). The sun going down at noon, and the earth dark in broad daylight (Amos 8:9) would most certainly have **my** undivided attention. After the thick darkness happens, something equally unusual will take place. The moon will become as bright as the sun, and the sun will become seven times brighter (Isa.30:26).

Environmental pollution

The scientific community today is concerned about a so called 'green house effect', in which the effects of our own pollution cause a change to occur in the upper atmospheric layers that is somewhat like the glass windows in a greenhouse. The result is that the overall average temperature is increasing. Some of the pollutants that we release into the atmosphere don't dissipate as quickly as we might think. Fluorocarbons and aerosol propellants like freon, end up in the upper atmosphere and contribute to the global thermal greenhouse effect. I speculate that a nuclear war could drastically affect this upper atmosphere which acts as a huge filter. It may well be, that if this filter is destroyed, and the nuclear dust cloud settles, that the moon and the sun would appear significantly brighter.

The explosion

Several portions of scripture seem to indicate nuclear explosions by describing what happens to the earth.

Isa. 24:19,20

The earth is broken asunder,
the earth is split through,
the earth is shaken violently,
the earth reels to and fro like a drunkard and totters like a shack...

I have often wondered if the earth has a natural frequency that might begin oscillating from a harmonic resonance set in motion by sequential nuclear explosions.

The Lord is going to instantly punish all the nations that wage war against Jerusalem by causing a whirlwind, thunder, earthquake, loud noise, and a consuming fire (Isa.29:6,7).

Neutron bombs

There are several passages in the Bible that remind me of the effects of a neutron bomb with an intense beta nuclear radiation. "...they will look at one another in astonishment, their faces aflame" (Isa.13:8). "Behold they have become like stubble; fire burns them; they cannot deliver themselves from the power of the flame..." (Isa.47:14).

Zech.14:12

Now this will be the plague with which the Lord will strike all the peoples who have gone to war against Jerusalem; their flesh will rot while they stand on their feet, and their eyes will rot in their sockets, and their tongue will rot in their mouth.

Did the writers of 'Raiders of the Lost Arc' read this passage from Zechariah when they filmed the scene of 'the opening of the arc'?

Weapons for fuel

After the destruction of Gog and his armies on the mountains of Israel, the inhabitants of the cities of Israel will make fires with the spoil of weapons they collect from the fallen armies of Gog, and they will make fires of the weapons for seven years (Ezek.39:9,10). Many people have speculated that these weapons were made of a certain kind of compressed wood that burns for a long time. I suppose that is a possibility, but I think that in light of the material just covered about the use of nuclear weapons, it seems a likelihood that the weapons gathered will really be portable short range nuclear field pieces which could be dismantled and the fissionable material used to fuel a nuclear reactor. The United States currently has an arsenal of 155mm shells that can be armed with nuclear warheads, and have a range of 18 to 20 miles. It seems incredible that a nuclear device could fit into a 6 inch diameter shell, but they do.

Gog's cemetery

After the smoke has cleared, and the Lord has been established as Messiah, they will appoint a burial plot for Gog and his army where they will be buried, and they will call it 'the valley of Hammon Gog'. (Ezek.39:11). Israel will be burying the army of Gog for 7 months. There has been considerable speculation concerning this 7 month burial time by different prophetic writers, and it may not really be completely understood until the time actually arrives. Because they go through the land burying the dead for seven months to 'cleanse' the land, has caused some to consider this to be a preparation for a future passover. If my speculations are correct, it has nothing to do with passover, but rather the cleansing is from radioactive physical remains of the destroyed army that was hit by neutron bombs which were detonated above ground level. The extended length of time for burial is a result of the safety procedures and precautions that must be taken to dispose of nuclear waste material. Searchers will go through the area with geiger counter type sensors that will detect radioactive material, and they will set markers to indicate where the 'hot spots' are. Another squad of 'burriers' will go to the markers with the proper disposal equipment, remove the radioactive debris (bones and etc.), and place it in a nuclear waste dump, which will be called 'Hammon Gog' (Ezek. 39:14,15).

Fission and Fusion

2 Pet.3:12

> *Looking for and hastening the coming of the day of God, on account of which the heavens will be destroyed by burning, and the elements will melt with intense heat.*

Nuclear fission is a term used to describe the 'splitting' of an atom of an element such as the rather unstable isotope of Uranium [235]. When this isotope is subjected to a neutron bombardment, a neutron is absorbed into the atom, causing it to fragment into an atom of Barium, an atom of Krypton, 3 free neutrons, and the release of substantial energy. The three free neutrons can also strike three other isotopes of U^{235} in a 'chain reaction' which rapidly escalates until it reaches an explosive violence. When this reaction is uncontrolled and has sufficient mass, a nuclear explosion results.

Nuclear fusion is a term to describe the 'combining' of certain isotopes of the Hydrogen atom in such a manner as to form Helium and release substantial atomic energy. The United States exploded the first 'Hydrogen Bomb' on November 1, 1952 at Eniwetok atoll in the Pacific. This explosion precipitated the development of weapons that are so powerful it taxes our imagination to even contemplate their destructive force. The fuel for this 'thermo-nuclear' device is Hydrogen, one of the elements found in our atmosphere. The term 'heavens', mentioned (2Pet.3:12), could easily be understood as 'atmosphere', and the verse literally says, 'the heavens (atmosphere), being set on fire, will be dissolved'. The word for 'element'[1] literally means "...the basic elements from which everything in the natural world is made, and of which it is composed...", melts with intense heat of burning, and I think that's a pretty good description of both nuclear fission and nuclear fusion for a fisherman from the first century.

The Great War

It may well be that as the tribulation progresses, wars become increasingly prevalent, and trouble in Israel escalates to a fever pitch in a physical warfare, that the Church will be engaged in spiritual warfare that escalates to a fever pitch also. There isn't any question as to the fact that in the last days, things will progress from bad to worse and from worse to catastrophic. Anyone who believes the world is going to get better and better has either never read any Biblical prophecy or does not consider the scripture literal. In either case, it is a serious mistake to make assumptions that are diametrically opposite to the clear teaching of the Word of God. There are several specific things that we are informed about that directly affect the church and the climate of the believer's spiritual warfare.

* 1.) Satan is cast out of heaven at about the middle of the tribulation period. (Rev. 12:9).

* 2.) Satan will come with wrath (Rev.12:12).
We are told that Satan is like a roaring lion seeking who he may devour (1 Peter 5:8) at the present time. What must he be like after being booted out of heaven?

* 3.) Evil men will progress from bad to worse (2Tim.3:13) and there will be an increase in crime and violence.

* 4.) Hedonism will prevail (2Tim.3:2). The soft church of America better be wary of this one, because they are not used

---

[1] ***στοιχεια***, Arndt & Ging. pg.776

to suffering hardship. An attitude of self satisfaction will prevail, and a weak church could easily fall victim in this area.

While Israel is waging a physical warfare with Satan and his forces led by the Antichrist, the church may well be waging a spiritual war with his forces led by fallen angels or (demons). This is no time for the Church to have a 'cocky' attitude about the Devil, and it most certainly is no time for the Church to be 'comatose'. Paul says that one of the very reasons that the 'falling away' or apostasy will occur **within** the Church, is because believers will be paying attention to 'deceitful spirits' and 'doctrines of demons' (1Tim.4:1). 'Listen up' you born again believers, I'm giving you a flat out warning. Either prepare yourself as a soldier while you still have the opportunity, (see Eph.6), or you are going to become a casualty.

American Idolatry

America is an idolatrous nation. Idolatry? Isn't that practiced in backwards countries where wooden images of animals are carved and then worshiped as a god? Yes, it could be, but idolatry is more than just an idol made from stone or wood or some other material, crafted by some artisan. Idolatry is really placing something ahead of God in a spiritual position where He is suppose to be.

Ezek.14:4

> *Therefore speak to them and tell them, 'Thus says the Lord God, Any man of the house of Israel who sets up his idols in his heart, puts right before his face the stumbling block of his iniquity...*

Notice where the idols are set up? In the heart. Now suppose an image was created of the thing that you daydream about, and dwell upon. If this image was placed on the mantle over your fireplace, it would be considered an idol by any of the backward countries that practice idolatry.

Col.3:5

Therefore consider the members of your earthly body as dead to immorality, impurity, passion, evil desire, and greed, which amounts to idolatry.

We are a greedy, self centered, hedonistic, amoral nation of sinners. Why should we even expect not to be judged by God? We are a diseased society plunging headlong into a quagmire of social depravation and spiritual malaise. Shall not the judge of all the earth do right?

Will Christians be judged too?

The real question is not whether God will judge sin or not, but the age old question is, 'will the righteous be judged with the wicked?', and the answer is equally ancient. Abraham questioned the Lord on this very point nearly 4000 years ago.

Gen.18:23

"...wilt thou indeed sweep away the righteous with the wicked?"

Recorded in the succeeding verses, we have one of the most interesting dialogues to be found anywhere in the Bible. God first revealed to Abraham that He was about to judge Sodom and Gomorrah because of their exceeding great sin, and then permits Abraham to haggle with Him concerning the righteous in Sodom. Abraham was concerned for the sake of his nephew Lot who was living there with his wife and two daughters, and perhaps he had some rapport with the kings of Sodom, since he had saved him and his people at the battle of 9 kings,(Gen.14).

God sometimes does permit mankind to alter the outcome of history, through intercessory prayer. It is incredible to even imagine that the Almighty would relegate the outcome of history to the intercessory prayer of godly men, but He has. Abraham haggled with God for 50, 45, 30, 20, and finally for 10 righteous people, until God said "I will not destroy it (Sodom) on account of ten" (Gen.18:32), and then stopped talking to him. Subsequently in Gen 19:29, God remembered Abraham, and sent Lot out of the midst of the city when he overthrew Sodom and Gomorrah. "...the effective prayer of a righteous man can accomplish much." (James 5:17). Before Sodom and Gomorrah were destroyed, the righteous were removed, with the exception of Lot's wife who looked back and became a pillar of salt. Lot didn't really want to leave the city very badly, and the angels had to literally seize his hand and lead him out of the city. When Lot approached his sons-in-law to get out of the city with him, they thought he was jesting. The world today hasn't changed much because it still mocks the righteous and thinks he is joking when he says destruction is coming. The angels of judgement couldn't accomplish their job until Lot was removed from the city, nevertheless they sternly warned Lot to get out lest he too be swept away in the city's judgement (Gen.19:15). It is very significant to this illustration, that the righteous in the city were given a prophetic warning that the city was to suffer impending catastrophic judgement through the agency of a messenger from God. Some have used this as a proof text to demonstrate that the rapture will occur before the tribulation, and we also maintain that God has, in fact, promised that His people would not be judged and condemned by His wrath, but rather delivered from it. (1 Thes.1:10; 1Thes.5:9; 2 Thes.3:3; Rom.5:9; Rom.1:18). However, these scriptures do not teach that the church must be 'raptured' prior to the time the Lord returns. All they are saying is that the Church will not undergo the wrath of God.

Two things that impressed me about the judgement on Sodom and Gomorrah is 1.) the effect that intercessory prayer played in the removal of the righteous, and 2.) there was a warning by a messenger of God prior to the judgement. When Jerusalem will be judged at the end of the tribulation, Jeremiah records that the Lord said '...If you can find a man, if there is one who does justice, who seeks truth, then I will pardon her.' And, of course, there are none! Even though they were religious and had all the right 'lingo', they were swearing falsely. They were 'religious fakes'.

Will the Church be called to arms?

Another question that comes up concerning America, and the church, is 'Will the church be sent to fight along with Christ in the last battle'? I don't believe so, because the angels are given some of that responsibility (Jude 14,15; 2Thes.1:7,8), and some of it is done alone by the Lord Himself (Isa.63:3). We will have more than enough warfare with the impending spiritual struggle with the Devil.

Say what?

The economists say we need fiscal reform.
The politicians say we need more tax revenues.
The aids victims say we need federal funded medical attention.
The gay rights people say we need more laws to protect them from the non gays.
The blacks say they need more 'freedom' which has a varied definition depending on the situation.
The teachers, in the midst of declining educational institutions, say they need more money. More funds is the typical solution for a quality education, where our inner city children get shot and killed in the playground by other students who carry lethal weapons. Ironically, educational standards of excellence in Japan and Europe are increasingly becoming superior to ours.
The local city and municipal governments need higher taxes to keep our streets and sidewalks paved, to fight crime, and protect our homes from fires.
The local police say then need more officers.
The residents say they need more protection from hooligans.
The automobile companies say we need to restrict Japanese and European auto imports that are increasingly being pur chased by the American car buyer who is seeking better values for the buck.

Crime has increased substantially; taxes have become a standing joke; the federal government continues to add an increasing volume of paychecks to an already over burdened payroll; more sex education is advocated as a solution to the problem of aids, unwanted babies, and venereal diseases; children are exposed to an ever increasing amount of promiscuity and lascivious television programming. Our 'pedal to the metal' fast lane society suffers the effects of malnutrition, while we spend more and more on fast foods and junk snacks. Can our failing society be salvaged, or is it hopelessly doomed to a downward spiral of the malaise of the 'American Way'?

Who is to be blamed?

Who, after all, is really to blame for the decline of this great nation? Dope addicts that bring crack into the school yard? Organized crime that brings cocaine to the wealthy as well as the poor? Lawyers who encourage lawsuits on doctors, whose malpractice insurance requires him to substantially increase his prices to offset the extra insurance expenses? Politicians who squeeze the lifeblood out of the middle class by never ending increase in the taxes? The Federal Government that absolutely must form another committee to determine how it can restructure the income tax to claim a tax reduction, while at the same time extract more funds from taxpayers? We may not need to worry about Russian ICBM's, we are so materialistic and worldly, we may spend ourselves to death.

Most of the suggestions to rectifying the quandary are temporary bandaids that treat symptoms rather than the disease. They humorously remind me of the fact that low humidity causes leather to shrink. I can easily demonstrate that self evident fact, because every winter when the air has less humidity, my belt shrinks one notch.

Is God really going to judge America? Are we really going to go through the tribulation? What are we supposed to do if that does happen?

2 Chron 7:13,14

If I shut up the heavens so that there is no rain,

> *or if I command the locust to devour the land, or if I send pestilence among My people, and My people who are called by My name humble themselves and pray, and seek My face and turn from their wicked ways, then I will hear from heaven, will forgive their sin, and will heal their land.*

There really is only one group of people that **can** make a difference in American, and there is only one group of people that are responsible for the condition that it is in - the people who are called by God's name. As CHRISTians we are the ones called by God's name, so whose fault is it that we are in the mess we are in? YEP! Us, the born again believers who have forgotten what it is to exercise our God given privilege of intercession on our knees, and who have forgotten what repentance is all about. As the cartoon 'Pogo' says, "We have met the enemy and he is us". To humble ourselves is to own up to our shortcomings, confess our sin and act responsibly toward God, the world, our nation, the church and our own family. Revival is not for the unbeliever who has nothing to revive, it is for believers who have gotten out of sync with God. Repentance is not just a simple confession of wrong doing, but a turning away from sin and a turning towards God in faith. They work together, hand in hand.

The promise of God to heal the land is contingent upon God's people doing these 4 things:

1.) Humbling themselves.
2.) Praying.
3.) Seeking God
4.) Turning from sin.

It all sounds too simple, doesn't it? Yet God has committed Himself to act in accordance with those stipulated conditions. All we need to do to receive the blessings of these verses, is to follow the directions He has specified. When is the last time you had a day of fasting and prayer just because you love the Lord, and want to get closer to Him? When is the last time you prayed for a spirit of revival and the spring rains of the Holy Spirit to be poured out upon the body of Christ? When have you EVER got down on your knees and beseeched the Lord to heal our land? If we made this a priority in our own lives and in the body collectively, we would see a change in our whole nation with respect to the quality of life. Is that all there is then? No!, that's just for starters. There is much we can do for God, for ourselves, for the body of Christ and for our country if we have the mind of Christ.

The promise of judgement

God **is** going to judge sin, and He **is** going to start with His own people in His own house.

1 Peter 4:17

> *For it is time for judgement to begin with the household of God; and if it begins with us first, what will be the outcome for those who do not obey the gospel of God?*

1 Cor.11:31

> *But if we judged ourselves rightly, we should not be judged.*

Either we are going to judge ourselves, or else we will be judged by God. There isn't any alternative. How are we to judge ourselves? The Church today is a mockery of what the Lord intended it to be, and is, for the most part, a disgrace and an embarrassment to the Lord. We think we know so much about spiritual things, but we really don't at all. In fact, most believers would be hard pressed to accurately define the nature of the body itself. The Church is NOT a denomination; it is NOT a building; it is NOT an organization. The Church is supposed to be like a living organism that must function as a unit to be healthy. Just like a human body, the body of Christ needs every part to be functioning properly and intra-dependant upon every other part to sustain itself.

We don't need to be 'mamby-pamby' milktoast christians that take a shot in the jaw by every dissident coming down the pike. We need to separate 'meekness' and 'weakness', and learn the difference between 'turning the other cheek' (Mt.5:3-9), and 'acting like men' (1 Cor.16:13).

Have you ever read Ephesians 6? Most readers will attest to the fact that they have a good knowledge of the contents of this chapter, and will not be surprised to learn that it contains a discussion on christian armor. Why do we need the 'full armor of God'? We need the armor, because we are right in the middle of a battle! Most of us aren't even aware that there is a war going on, let alone that we are right in the middle of a critical battle. We, as God's army, are in a warfare with Satan and his army, and "..our struggle is not against flesh and blood, but against the rulers, against the powers, against the world forces of this darkness, against the spiritual forces of wickedness in the heavenly places."(Eph.6:12). I know that some 'spiritual' christians are busy chasing Satan around, and that's not what I am talking about. When well meaning christians are always rebuking the devil, it's a pretty good indication that they are casualties in another area. What I mean is, that Satan is very sneaky and clever, and if he can convince us that our main confrontation is directly with him, he will plunder us indirectly. It's like a warfare on land, sea and air. When we think we have him beat on the ground, he sends a torpedo and sinks us anyway. We won't have victories all of the time. In fact, we may have few victories, but that doesn't preclude the fact that we are prepared and ready to do battle on every front, and cognizant of his schemes. A friend of mine recently told me that he thought that Satan was already cast down to the earth, and was surprised to learn that Satan still has access to the throne of God, where he accuses the brethren day and night. There is coming a day in the near future when that is going to change, and Satan will be kicked out of the presence of the Lord, and cast down to earth, where he will viciously attack God's people because he knows his time is short lived (Rev.12:12). As Christians, we need more than ever to re-evaluate what the scriptures tell us about ourselves. What we are, who we are and what our task is supposed to be, is significant, because if I understand the scripture correctly, we aren't even close. We need to re-examine the mandate that Jesus gave us (Mt.28:19,20) to go forth and make disciples of all nations, baptizing, and teaching, and implement it collectively in practical ways that are effective in getting the job done. Assuming that we have initiated the 4 steps listed in both our private lives, and within the body, and assuming that the 2nd Advent is at least a few years off, there are some things that we can do to implement some of the things we are 'supposed' to accomplish, and I'm going to list just a few:

*** *Stewardship judgement***

I never fail to be amazed at how many TV evangelists that 'God' has told to deliver a message about tithing to their organization, and I never fail to be amazed at how many people comply and send in their money. Stewardship is one of the primary areas where we need to exercise self judgement. I am frankly embarrassed that the Body of Christ spends so much of its funds on entertainment and dumb projects to satiate the ego of some self appointed 'gurus' of the faith, and then have the audacity to call it 'evangelism'. I see 'men of God' pleading for funds in a manner that reminds me of a carnival barker with a straw hat and cane trying to con people into participation in a 'no win' game. Instead of a dollar for 3 throws of a baseball to win a teddy bear, we are encouraged to send in a thousand dollars and have our name permanently inscribed on a brick in the new hotel, or the park's water slide. This is not what I call stewardship at all, and after reading Mt.21:12,13 where Jesus cast out the money changers in the temple, I'm pretty sure He wouldn't call it good stewardship either. We need to look again at what Jesus was talking about in all those parables that deal with stewardship, and about being unable to serve both God and Mammon (Mt.6:24). We need to support those who bless us spiritually, and by that I mean those that 'feed' us, not 'entertain' us. Perhaps we need to have some kind of agency to evaluate the authenticity and veracity of some of these 'worthwhile' projects.

*** Communication**

In this modern age of technology and computers we need to employ the tools that the world can furnish to our own advantage. We desperately need organization and communication to survive the onslaught of the end time conditions. We need an organization that is chain reactive without the encumbrance of a hierarchal power structure seeking its own recognition and authority. Local churches should have a sufficient network of communication so that the pastor could notify one other person about an assembly time and place, and have the whole congregation in attendance. Local churches need a network of communication to enable them to function as a unit and stand firm against the wiles of the Devil. A coalition of Evangelical local assemblies, with a minimum of structure, that can coordinate a mutual exchange of information and assistance, will become a necessity for the survival of the body through tribulation. The first church council in Jerusalem (Acts 15) had a coordinated relationship with the other churches that kept them on the same wavelength as the Holy Spirit. Sure we need to be 'independent', and sure we need to be 'separate' from the world, but that doesn't mean that we also have to be 'stupid'. A coordinated effort of Evangelicals could do much for influencing bills in Congress that directly relate to our philosophy and lifestyle. The age old adage that 'the squeaky wheel gets the oil' not only is true, but is the order of the day with the godless minority that have made their presence only too obvious from the supreme court decisions to the local government regulations to schoolboard decisions. Can you imagine The United States during World War II with no communications between the Air Force, Marines, Navy, and Army?

Can you imagine the outcome with no strategy, no coordinated Pacific effort, no plan for Normandy beach, and no general objectives? This may seem ludicrous, but the Church today is like a lot of small platoons of infantry soldiers with no supervision, no coordination, no weapons, and no goals. They wander around aimlessly, and more often than not are found fighting amongst themselves. They aren't able to even handle peace, let alone a battle for survival.

*** *Education***

We Christians have really back peddled in the area of education, and I know this is a touchy issue with so many people who have their children in 'christian schools', but I have to say it anyway. Instead of getting involved with the school board and 'duking it out', we take the shot on the jaw, back peddle, and say, 'well we will just have to start a christian school, because this secular education doesn't teach the right value system anymore'. The public educational system was originally started by Christian people with a desire to educate children, and I don't think we should relinquish what is ours to begin with, to a minority of worldly people who are wiser in their domain than we are. No sir! We need to 'storm the Bastille' and take back what we have lost. When the Word of God tells us to 'come out from among them, and be separate...', it is not encouraging us to fall back into some cloistered order, but rather to behave properly, as the Children of God, with a holy life that is pleasing to Him. The world is mocking us and taking advantage of us because we are such 'wimps', and we are either too dumb to realize it, or too spiritual to get involved. If you don't think the educational system is putting out an acceptable education for your children, then organize the Christians as a group, get some seats on the schoolboard (they have elections you know), and get the right material to the kids.

*** *Politics***

We complain, complain, complain about crooked politicians

that keep raising taxes and feathering their own nest, but we hardly ever see anybody that has guts enough to run for an office with Christian integrity. Why don't we as Christians vote for and elect a 'Christian' in politics? Oh sure, we like to see if there is one to vote for, but what about getting behind a Christian candidate who runs on integrity and canvass votes for him. We need to get involved with politics. Sure it's dirty business, but it's dirty business because we have let it get that way. I thank God that many of the men we have elected president in the past few years have been at least nominal christians, but perhaps we owe even that to those little old ladies who are always at the prayer meetings praying for our nation. Get involved with politics, we **can** make a difference!

**** Social Illness***

Why are we facing an Aids epidemic? If people were obeying God's moral directions there wouldn't be a problem with abortions, drugs, aids, and crime. People do these type of things because they either don't know what God says, or they don't care. Either way they need to know what God says about it. Dandy!! How do they learn about God? How will they hear, unless someone is sent, and how can they hear without someone to tell them? The Church has pulled out of the inner cities, and moved to the suburbs and left empty buildings where a life giving organism used to be. I include the Roman Catholic Church here also, even though we have many theological differences, there are some things that are right too. Paul said that whenever Christ is preached in pretence or in truth, he would rejoice (Phil.1:18). But, because the inner city churches weren't able to support themselves financially, the church closed its doors. That is just not right. We don't want to see the inner city infested with crime and drugs, but we aren't willing to keep the church open to them either. There is something basically wrong with the church when it pulls itself out of the inner city to avoid contact with black america, and then has the audacity to send missionaries to

South Africa. If your aren't willing to carry the cross, don't make the trip. We are so concerned about building our fancy church buildings that we don't realize that what we actually are doing is building walls to keep people out. We are told to go into the highways and byways, but we expect the sinners to show up at Sunday services and come to us. See, we have that turned around. We are supposed to go to them, because they don't even know that we have what they need. Instead of building bell towers, and monuments to personalities, it would be more in keeping to the command of Christ to build soup kitchens!

Ezek.34:14

> *"Those who are sickly you have not strengthened, the diseased you have not healed, the broken you have not bound up, the scattered you have not brought back, nor have you sought for the lost;..."*

Micah 5:15

> *and I will execute vengeance in anger and wrath on the nations which have not obeyed.*

Is America going to be judged? It all depends on us, and the jury is still out on that one.

BIBLIOGRAPHY

This is an expanded bibliography of the references found in the footnotes that were abbreviated for technical reasons. This list is not inclusive of the totality of books used in the research of this project, nor does it reflect my personal library. It is just an expansion of that which I have already referred to.

Arndt & Gingrich, *A Greek-English Lexicon,* a translation of Bauer, distributed by Zondervan, Grand Rapids :1957

Bagster,Samuel *The Analytical Greek Lexicon,* Harper and Row, New York. no copyright and no author listed. sometimes referred to as just 'Zondervan'.

Bremner, Paul,III, *Countering Terrorism in the 1980's and 1990's,* Department of State Bulletin, Feb. 1989.

Cairns, Earle, *Christianity Through the Centuries,* Zondervan, Grand Rapids:1954.

Compton's Encyclopedia, E.F.Compton, Chicago:1951.

Dana and Mantey, *A Manual Grammar of the Greek New Testament,* MacMillan Company, Toronto, Ontario:1927.

Davis Dictionary of the Bible, Royal Publishers,inc., Nashville:1973.

Encyclopedia of Asian History, vol.2, Collier Macmillian, London:1988.

Encyclopaedia Judaica, Keler Publishing House, Jerusalem:1972.

Eusebius, *The History of the Church from Christ to Constantine*, translated by G.A. Williamson, University Press, New York:1966.

Furneaux, Rupert, *The Roman Siege of Jerusalem,* David McKay Company, New York:1972.

Finnigan, Jack,*Light From the Ancient Past*, Princeton University Press, 1946,1959.

Gundry,Robert *The Church and the Tribulation*, Zondervan, Grand Rapids:1973.

Hislop,Alexander, *The Two Babylons*, A & C Black,Ltd. England:1916; Loizeau Brothers, New York :2nd Am. ed.1959.

Josephus, Flavius, *Complete Works*, translated by William Whiston, Kregel Publications, Grand Rapids:1964.

Kraeling, Emil G., *Bible Atlas*, Rand McNally, New York:1957

Ladd, George, *The Blessed Hope*, Eerdmans, Grand Rapids:1956.

Larkin, Clarence, *Dispensational Truth*, self published:1918

MacPherson, Dave, *The Incredible Cover-Up*, Logos International, Plainfield, N.J.:1975.

Bibliography

Pentecost,Dwight J. *Prophecy For Today*, Zondervan, Grand Rapids:1961.

Pfeiffer, Charles, *The Biblical World*, Baker, Grand Rapids:1966.

Ramm, Bernard, *Protestant Biblical Interpretation*, W.A. Wilde Company, Boston:1956

Tatford, Fredrick A., *The Climax of the Ages*, Zondervan, Grand Rapids:1953.

The International Standard Bible Encyclopedia, Eerdmans, Grand Rapids:1960. (abreviated as I.S.B.E. in text).

The New International Version, Zondervan, Grand Rapids:1973. (sometimes abreviated as N.I.V.).

The New Standard Jewish Encyclopedia, Doubleday & Co, Garden City,NY:1970.

The Oxford Annotated Apocrypha, Revised Standard Version, Oxford University Press, N.Y.:1965.

Thomas, Raymond, *America and After In Prophecy*, The Word and Times Press, (East Detroit:no date) c. 1973.

Unger, Merrill F., *Unger's Bible Dictionary*, Moody Press, Chicago:1961.

VanBaalen, J.K., *The Chaos of Cults*, Wm.B.EerdmansPublishingCo.,GrandRapids:1938,51,56,60,62.

Walvoord,John F., *The Rapture Question*, Zondervan, Grand Rapids:1957.

ORDER FORM

Copies of this book may be purchased by mail directly from the publisher by mailing this completed form with the correct amount to:

EPIPHANY PUBLICATIONS
P.O. Box 721271
BERKLEY, MI. 48072

Please send me the following items checked or numbered below:

☐ copies of ***THE LAST TRUMP*** at $8.95 each, plus $1.00 each for shipping and handling. 5 or more less %20.

☐ please put me on the mailing list to recieve the ***Epiphany Bulletin,*** a quarterly Epiphany newsletter. at $2.00 per year (cost of printing and mailing).

☐ I want to know more about being ready for the LORDS return, and what it means to 'be saved'. Please send me some helpful literature.

☐ I would like further information pertaining to the possiblility of obtaining H.L. McLean as a guest speaker/teacher on prophecy.
contact me (name)______________________________
at ph.#________________________

please mail books and/or items checked above to:

name____

address____

city____

zip____

ORDER FORM

Copies of this book may be purchased by mail directly from the publisher by mailing this completed form with the correct amount to:

EPIPHANY PUBLICATIONS
P.O. Box 721271
BERKLEY, MI. 48072

Please send me the following items checked or numbered below:

☐ copies of ***THE LAST TRUMP*** at $8.95 each, plus $1.00 each for shipping and handling. 5 or more less %20.

☐ please put me on the mailing list to recieve the ***Epiphany Bulletin,*** a quarterly Epiphany newsletter. at $2.00 per year (cost of printing and mailing).

☐ I want to know more about being ready for the LORDS return, and what it means to 'be saved'. Please send me some helpful literature.

☐ I would like further information pertaining to the possiblility of obtaining H.L. McLean as a guest speaker/teacher on prophecy.
contact me (name)____________________________
at ph.#________________________

please mail books and/or items checked above to:

name____

address______________________________________

city____

zip____

ORDER FORM

Copies of this book may be purchased by mail directly from the publisher by mailing this completed form with the correct amount to:

EPIPHANY PUBLICATIONS
P.O. Box 721271
BERKLEY, MI. 48072

Please send me the following items checked or numbered below:

☐ copies of ***THE LAST TRUMP*** at $8.95 each, plus $1.00 each for shipping and handling. 5 or more less %20.

☐ please put me on the mailing list to recieve the ***Epiphany Bulletin,*** a quarterly Epiphany newsletter. at $2.00 per year (cost of printing and mailing).

☐ I want to know more about being ready for the LORDS return, and what it means to 'be saved'. Please send me some helpful literature.

☐ I would like further information pertaining to the possiblility of obtaining H.L. McLean as a guest speaker/teacher on prophecy.
contact me (name)______________________________
at ph.#__________________________

please mail books and/or items checked above to:

name____

address____

city____

zip____